Authors
Alejandra Aguado, Tabitha Barber,
Maria Bilske, David Blayney Brown,
Helen Delaney, Robin Hamlyn,
Karen Hearn, Andreas Leventis,
Elizabeth Manchester, Martin Myrone,
Martin Postle, Alison Smith,
Robert Upstone, Ian Warrell

The 100 artworks illustrated in this guide cover 500 years
of British history. From Hogarth to Turner, from Gainsborough
to Francis Bacon and Damien Hirst, the vitality and quality
of British art across the centuries shines out from the works
of the nation's most famous artists. With a penetrating
introduction by Martin Myrone and informative entries
for each work, this is a concise and accessible introduction
to British art.

Tate Britain
100 works from the Tate Collection

1500

John Bettes
A Man in a Black Cap
1545

Marcus Gheeraerts II
Portrait of an Unknown Lady
c.1595

1600

Anon, British School
The Cholmondeley Ladies
c.1600–10

1700

James Thornhill
Design for Invitation Card…
1718

Philip Mercier
The Schutz Family and their Friends on a Terrace
1725

John Vanderbank
Equestrian Design…
1728

Andrea Soldi
Portrait of Henry Lannoy Hunter in Oriental Dress…
c.1733–6

Allan Ramsay
Thomas, 2nd Baron Mansel of Margam…
1742

William Hogarth
The Painter and his Pug
1745

George Stubbs
Reapers
1785

James Barry
King Lear Weeping over the Dead Body of Cordelia
1786–8

William Blake
Elohim Creating Adam
1795/c.1805

Henry Fuseli
The Shepherd's Dream, from 'Paradise Lost'
1786

1800

Th…
La…
M…
18…

J.M.W. Turner
Venice: The Giudecca Canal, Looking towards Fusina at Sunset
1840

J.M.W. Turner
Snow Storm: Hannibal and his Army Crossing the Alps
exh 1812

John Everett Millais
Christ in the House of His Parents…
1849–50

John Martin
The Plains of Heaven
1851–3

John Constable
Flatford Mill ('Scene on a Navigable River')
1816–17

Henry W…
Chatterton
1856

Frederic, Lord Leighton
And the Sea Gave up the Dead Which Were in It
exh 1892

John Singer Sargent
W. Graham Robertson
1894

1900

Walter Richard Sickert
La Hollandaise
c.1906

Wyndham Lewis
Workshop
c.1914–15

Duncan Grant
The Tub
c.1913

Jacob Epstein
Torso in Metal from 'The Rock Drill'
1913–14

Stanley Swan
Swar…
1915–

Francis Bacon
Three Studies for Figures at the Base of a Crucifixion
c.1944

Barbara Hepworth
Group I (Concourse) February 4 1951
1951

John Latham
Belief System
1959

Peter Lanyon
Thermal
1960

Anthony Caro
Early One Morning
1962

Phillip King
Tra-La-La
1963

Bridget Riley
Fall
1963

Richard Long
Red Slate Circle
1988

Patrick Caulfield
After Lunch
1975

Howard Hodgkin
Dinner at Smith Square
1975–9

Bill Woodrow
Twin-Tub with Guitar
1981

Tony Cragg
Axehead
1982

Richard Deacon
For Those Who Have Ears #2
1983

Anish Kapoor
As if to Celebrate, I Discovered a Mountain…
1981

Tracey Emin
Outside Myself …
1995

Susan Hiller
From the Freud Museum
1991–6

Sarah Lucas
Pauline Bunny
1997

Angela Bulloch
West Ham – Sculpture for Football Songs
1998

2000

Tacita Dean
Palast
2004

Steve McQueen
Caribs' Leap/Western Deep
2002

Rosalind Nashashibi
Hreash House
2004

Richard Wentworth
Making Do…
1974–2005
Occasional Geometries
1973–2005

Jeremy Deller
The Battle of Orgreave Archive…
2004

Tomma Abts
Noeme
2004

Gilb…
Fate
200…

Nathaniel Bacon
Cookmaid with
Still Life of
Vegetables and
Fruit c.1620–5

Francis Cleyn
Samuel's
Reproach to Saul
c.1630–5

David des
Granges
The Saltsonstall
Family
c.1640

William Dobson
Endymion Porter
c.1642–5

Francis Hayman
Samuel
Richardson,
the Novelist
(1684–1761)...
1740–1

Jan Siberechts
View of a House
and its Estate
in Belsize,
Middlesex 1696

ough
nell

rokatt

Johan Zoffany
Three Sons of
John, 3rd Earl
of Bute c.1763–4

Joshua
Reynolds
Colonel Acland
and Lord
Sydney: The
Archers 1769

Joseph Wright
of Derby
An Iron Forge
1772

Richard Wilson
Llyn-y-Cau,
Cader Idris
?exhibited 1774

Thomas Jones
An Excavation
of an Antique
Building in
a Cava ?1777,
later dated 1779

John Singleton
Copley
The Death of
Major Peirson,
6 January 1781
1783

David Wilkie
The Village
Holiday
1809–11

John Linnell
Kensington
Gravel Pits
1811–12

John Downman
Thomas
Williams,
a Black Sailor
1815

Richard Parkes
Bonington
French Coast
with Fishermen
1826

Samuel Palmer
Coming from
Evening Church
1830

J.M.W. Turner
Norham Castle,
Sunrise
c.1845

William Dyce
Pegwell Bay, Kent
– a Recollection
of October
5th 1858
?1858–60

James Abbott
McNeill
Whistler
Symphony
in White,
No.2...1864

Dante Gabriel
Rossetti
The Beloved
('The Bride')
1865–6

John Frederick
Lewis
The Siesta
1876

Edward
Coley
Burne-
Jones
The Golden
Stairs 1880

John William
Waterhouse
The Lady
of Shalott
1888

Harry Bates
Pandora
exh 1891

dward
urra
he Snack
ar
930

Ben Nicholson
1935
(White Relief)
1935

Henry Moore
Recumbent
Figure
1938

Graham
Sutherland
Green Tree
Form: Interior
of Woods
1940

Paul Nash
Totes Meer
(Dead Sea)
1940–1

nore

en,

and

Gustav
Metzger
Liquid Crystal
Environment
1965–6

Barry
Flanagan
Four Casb
2 '67
1967

Richard
Hamilton
Swingeing
London 67 (f)
1968–9

Hamish Fulton
The Pilgrims'
Way
1971

Bruce McLean
Pose Work
for Plinths 3
1971

Parker
eces

Damien Hirst
Pharmacy
1992

Mona Hatoum
Incommunicado
1993

Antony
Gormley
Testing a
World View
1993

Douglas
Gordon
10ms-1
1994

eed
232:
e World
rk = the
orld

Rachel
Whiteread
Untitled (Stairs)
2001

Chris Ofili
The Upper Room
1999–2002

Jim Lambie
Zobop
2003

Mark Wallinger
Sleeper
2004–5

Ceal Floyer
Double Act
2006

Tate Britain
100 works from the
Tate Collection

Tate Publishing

First published 2007 by order of the Tate Trustees
by Tate Publishing, a division of Tate Enterprises Ltd,
Millbank, London SW1P 4RG
www.tate.org.uk/publishing

© Tate 2007

British Library Cataloguing in Publication Data
A catalogue record for this book is available from the British Library

ISBN: 978 1 85437 745 6

Library of Congress Cataloging in Publication Data
Library of Congress Control Number: 2007924373

Designed by Jon Hill Design & Art Direction
Printed in Spain by Grafos S.A.

Measurements of artworks are given in centimetres, height before width.

BP British Art Displays

Supported by BP

Foreword
Stephen Deuchar

The works of art featured in this book form part of Tate's British Collections, which are given focus in the annual BP British Art Displays at Tate Britain, presented free of admission charge to the public. Individual works are sometimes included in or lent to special exhibitions elsewhere, of course, and modern and contemporary British works in the Collection are also shown at Tates Modern, Liverpool and St Ives. These changing contexts allow us regularly to review and refresh our appreciation of individual works and cumulatively to form an ever-deepening understanding of the various narratives and characteristics of British art itself.

Tate Britain emerged in 2000 in parallel with the opening of Tate Modern, successors together of the original Tate Gallery founded in 1897 by Henry Tate. Since then Tate Britain's role as the national gallery of British art has, I believe, happily fulfilled the founder's original intention to see 'the national school' properly celebrated. But our programme of displays, exhibition and interpretation has also raised questions about the very nature and parameters of British art, undermining some of those comfortable old certainties about its scope, style and identity which may once have prevailed. This has been a positive and, indeed, often exhilarating process. Through the medieval sculpture project *Image and Idol* in 2001, for example, we acknowledged that the story of British art really started much earlier than the date of the earliest work in the Collection (John Bettes's *A Man in a Black Cap* of 1545) and, through the involvement of the artist Richard Deacon in the process of selecting and displaying the works in the exhibition, we proposed the rich potential of ranging on occasion across swathes of time rather than considering all works exclusively in the context of their historical moment.

Our programme of thematic exhibitions has also mined some new seams in the history of British art: *Exposed: the Victorian Nude* (2001) and *Gothic Nightmares: Fuseli, Blake and the Romantic Imagination* (2006), for example, both shed fresh light on familiar subject matter, and a sequence of shows exploring the relationship between British and French art – *Constable to Delacroix* (2003), *Turner Whistler Monet* (2005), and *Degas, Sickert and Toulouse-Lautrec* (2005–6) demonstrated the remarkable permeability of national boundaries, at least when drawn in the visual arts.

The rich rewards of questioning and reconsidering traditional assumptions about British art have inspired our historic programme since 2000, leading to pioneering reappraisals of, amongst others, William Hogarth, Thomas

Opposite:
Image and Idol 2001
Installation at Tate Britain

6

Gainsborough, Joshua Reynolds and Stanley Spencer. This has been complemented by a series of significant presentations of the work of living British artists, which in most cases have for the first time set out a full account of their complete careers to date. There have been major retrospectives of the work of Lucian Freud, Bridget Riley, Anthony Caro and Howard Hodgkin, as well as surveys of the work of younger artists such as Tacita Dean and Wolfgang Tillmans. And we have established the Tate Triennial, a major periodic analysis of new developments in British art, supported by Art Now, a programme of small-scale projects in which emerging British artists are shown at Tate for the first time, often to appear subsequently, it has transpired, on the shortlists for our perennially popular annual Turner Prize.

Our ambition to present and analyse a broad range of new work, and to encourage general debate about the contemporary visual arts in Britain, has also been expressed in the four major commissions we have so far made for the Duveen Galleries, the grand public space which runs from one end of Tate Britain's main building to the other. These commissions have ranged from Mona Hatoum's disconcerting *The Entire World as a Foreign Land* (2000) to the deeply affecting personal essay that was Michael Landy's *House* (2004). Anya Gallaccio's *Beat* (2002–3) was a provocative exploration of Tate's Britishness, and Mark Wallinger's *State Britain* (2007) famously brought contemporary politics into the very heart of our collection displays.

Indeed the relationship between the visual arts and the perpetual national debate about the changing nature and nuances of Britishness is one which Tate Britain's programme has sought to explore at many levels. In 2003, for instance, we mounted a special display, *Inventing Britain*, addressing aspects of Welsh, Scottish, Irish and English identity with particular reference to France. Recently the focus has centred more determinedly on the broad cultural make-up of the British population as a whole and the question of how identities are enshrined. Displays such as *Seeing Africa* (2006) and *East-West* (2006–7) made stimulating contributions to this debate, followed by the programme assembled for our 2008 presentation of British Orientalist painting and photography. It is both the responsibility and the privilege of our curatorship here to animate Tate's British Collection with authority and rigour, but also to do so within an open and questioning frame of mind, alert to the multifaceted role of British art across six centuries in defining the culture of Britain today.

Stephen Deuchar
Director, Tate Britain

Introduction
Martin
Myrone

The five hundred years of British art represented in Tate's permanent Collection encompass works that may inspire, move and sometimes surprise. Even in the relatively restricted selection of one hundred images illustrated here, the vitality and quality of British art across the centuries should be apparent in the works of the nation's most famous artists, from Hogarth to Turner and Rossetti, and in the twentieth century from Stanley Spencer and Jacob Epstein to Bridget Riley and Lucian Freud. The landscape paintings of Gainsborough and Constable, the meticulous creations of the Pre-Raphaelites and the penetrating figure studies of Bacon and Hockney provide some of the most familiar images in the Western tradition. In the field of contemporary art the diverse and sometimes challenging nature of current practice is demonstrated here through works by Jeremy Deller, Chris Ofili and Martin Creed. They deploy a dizzying array of media to explore pressing questions of politics, identity and cultural value, often with a share of humour and no small degree of daring.

Together, these one hundred works, spanning the period from the middle of the sixteenth century to the present day, illustrate the manifold shifts in technique, subject matter, style and ambition that have been the traditional focus of art historians and critics. They may also reveal much more about the changing role and purpose of visual art, and still more about the world these objects were created in and the cultures that have played host to them since – including, importantly, our own. They are testament to the historical transformations that saw the peoples of the British Isles consolidate, uneasily, into a nation, and move from a relatively marginal place within Europe to become the first great capitalist economy and the head of the vastest empire ever known – a story of heroism and adventure, certainly, but also of violence, corruption and the basest exploitation. They mark, in sometimes explicit and sometimes indirect ways, the wars and social change, industrial revolution and economic decline that have subsequently shaped Britain's history. And they bear witness to the successive waves of migration and immigration and the fractious politics and religious life that have reshaped the identities of the peoples of Britain over these centuries, even as international conflicts and political coercion have sometimes helped the advance of a more stringent and exclusive sense of national identity.

The increasing wealth of Britain's social elite is manifested in the splendour and diversity of the art that was commissioned from the late seventeenth century onwards, as the old propertied classes were joined – and rivalled by –

William Hogarth
O The Roast Beef of Old England
('The Gate of Calais') 1748
Oil on canvas
78.8 x 94.5
Tate. Presented by the Duke of Westminster
1895

merchants and professionals, and as the culture of the great cities grew more cosmopolitan. The commercial vigour of the art market is apparent in the proliferation of talents during the nineteenth century, as a new breed of patrons emerged among the industrial elite, and as an ever-broadening audience for art helped raise artists to a level of fame and fortune that had never been known before. With world wars and social change in the twentieth century, new ideas about art and the social role of the artist appeared, and were variously embraced and rejected in an increasingly fragmented art world. The peculiar vitality and global visibility of British culture as a whole from the 1960s onwards – the accompaniment to the decline of real political power and economic and imperial influence – can be traced here, too. Today, British artists have a particular and arguably unprecedented place in the international scene, and Britain itself is a magnet for creative individuals around the world, creating a heady cultural mix.

John Constable
A Cornfield ?1817
Oil on canvas
61.3 x 51
Tate. Accepted by HM Government in lieu of
Inheritance Tax and allocated to Tate 2004

The sheer variety of works in the present selection would confound attempts to imagine a coherent tradition of British art that imposed an overarching national narrative joining together all these artists and eras in a simple fashion. Certainly, it may be possible to detect recurring tendencies and qualities that manifest themselves over generations, even over centuries. But efforts to match the changing styles and subject matter of British art to a singular national temperament, or to relate these too mechanistically to historical shifts, have rarely been successful; British art has always been too greatly marked by contradiction and paradox.

To cultural critics and commentators of the sixteenth, seventeenth and earlier eighteenth centuries Britain's visual arts lagged behind that of Continental Europe to an embarrassing degree. While Italy and France, the Netherlands and Holland, even Germany and Spain, had produced masters, Britain had none. The British art world was full of painters born abroad rather than on native soil: the multitudes of Dutch and Flemish artists who came in the seventeenth century, such as Jan Siberechts; or French and Italian artists such as Benedetto Gennari. What patronage there was stemmed largely from a property-owning elite not known for its progressive cultural tastes. Various excuses and explanations circulated: in the damp air and poor light of the north artists could not be properly inspired as they were by the golden environment of the Mediterranean; because of the religious reformation and civil wars of the sixteenth and seventeenth centuries, the arts were not nurtured by the Church and monarchy as they were abroad; and the imperial conquests and international commerce that fuelled Britain's economy did not provide the right stimulus for creativity. Yet amid the preponderance of foreign-born talent there were important native artists: John Bettes, whose Holbein-style portrait is the earliest work in the Collection; William Dobson, who adopted Van Dyck's style and adapted it for a court-in-exile during the civil wars of the mid-seventeenth century; and the idiosyncratic, aristocratic amateur, Nathaniel Bacon. More generally, historians have become aware that there were many more, and better-employed, painters of British extraction at work in London and in other cities by the later seventeenth century.

In the following century the wealth and material splendour of the nation increased enormously, fuelled by industrial enterprise and international trade – not least the hugely risky but vastly profitable, transatlantic traffic in African slaves and the investments in the sugar plantations on which they laboured. For the first time a distinctively British art scene took shape, primarily in London but also in Edinburgh and Glasgow, Dublin and York, and many other urban centres around the country. Foremost among these artists were Francis Hayman, the painter of portraits and literary scenes, and William Hogarth, whose richly detailed and comic representations of contemporary life were acclaimed not just by his contemporaries but by future generations and, importantly, foreign critics. Their work reflected an unruly culture of enterprise, which was riven by professional rivalries and the constant fight for patronage but gave birth to proudly patriotic artistic ideals and competing calls for some kind of national, institutional focus for the arts. Such an organisation would help ensure that Britain's cultural achievements in this field could match its achievements in the great imperial wars and commercial conquests of mid-

century, most significantly the Seven Years War (1756–63), which established the global pre-eminence of British naval power. Something like this arrived in 1768, in the form of a new Royal Academy of Arts in London. The Academy's close associations with the crown, metropolitan bias and idealistic insistence on the academic study of the human body and the production of high-minded narrative pictures, rather than more practical concerns, were highly divisive. The optimists had hoped that the Academy would help Britain become like ancient Greece or Rome, or Renaissance Italy, the home of great artists working in splendour, adored by princes and worshipped by an enlightened public. Nothing of the sort emerged. The new annual exhibitions, held from 1780 in splendid purpose-built rooms in Somerset House on the Strand, were dominated by portraits, landscapes and sentimental scenes. Where artists did take up grand literary themes, they did so in the service of commercial paymasters like the entrepreneur John Boydell, who commissioned James Barry's *Lear and Cordelia*, or produced works that seemed dangerously eccentric, such as those by Henry Fuseli or William Blake, both of whom were dismissed as being simply mad.

The period from the middle of the eighteenth to the mid-nineteenth century has, nonetheless, traditionally been considered as a 'golden age' of British art. These claims have been made largely on the basis of the highly original landscape paintings and naturalistic portraiture of these decades. The intense nature studies of John Constable and John Linnell, and the epic paintings of J.M.W. Turner, have provided a lastingly powerful idea of the British landscape, while Thomas Lawrence's flamboyantly painted portraits encapsulate an enduring ideal of fleshly glamour. The remarkable career of Turner, the son of a barber who rose to become one of the most successful and acclaimed artists of his day, is testament to an art world full of opportunity, driven by chance and by complex market conditions. Yet this golden age of British art was underpinned by a history of war – with revolutionary America (1775–83) and France and her allies (1793–1815) – and turbulent politics that rarely surfaces in the art itself but had a vital role to play in shaping its values and qualities. The intense study of the native landscape and expressive painting techniques developed among artists over these years were considered by the growing body of the culturally literate, middle-class public to embody peculiarly national characteristics, and gained additional meaning in the context of the wider conflicts and anxieties that threatened their interests.

While the audience for art flourished as the nineteenth century progressed, the continued lack of state support for the arts and the evident failings of the art education system (despite repeated attempts at reform) seemed to suggest that things had not changed so greatly. The industrial-scale manufacture of printed reproductions of paintings, new art magazines and the 'Art Unions', which raffled pictures to their many thousands of subscribers, helped constitute a genuinely mass market for art and promised unprecedented material rewards for artists. But for many critics the artists of the time pandered too often to public taste for the trite and sentimental, their techniques were corrupt, and their vision was sapped by their material successes. In the 1820s Samuel Palmer and the artists known as the 'Ancients', united in their admiration of William Blake, looked back to medieval art as a source of inspiration, while the later generation of Pre-Raphaelites, including, notably, the youthful John Everett Millais, hoped that by banding together in artistic brotherhood and imitating the techniques of the fifteenth- and sixteenth-century masters they could counter the prevailing influence of the market. The nostalgia expressed in their work echoes the disenchantment experienced by many highly educated artists across Europe at this time. By contrast, the apocalyptic visions of John Martin, a working-class painter who lacked academic training, played to the popular taste for spectacle, to a degree considered degrading and sensationalist by the snootier sort of critic.

For all the diversity of ideas about culture in the later nineteenth century, and the palpable material success and acclaim of so many artists, there was a persistent sense that modern British art was a problem and that the taste of the public was corrupted or inadequate. Among reformers like John Ruskin and William Morris, the writers who were formulating for the first time a comprehensive history of British art, and the progressive artists of the Pre-Raphaelite Brotherhood (formed in 1848) and latterly the New English Art Club (founded 1886), the relationships between industry, commerce and art, popular taste and elite critical opinion, the past and the present were enduring problems. In France these debates were accompanied by the famous emergence of artistic bohemia and concerted efforts to challenge a stultifying art establishment. The stark contests between state-sponsored academic artists and progressive painters, who served a specifically bourgeois market and the accompanying system of art dealers, never gained such clarity in a British context. The anachronistic qualities and lack of aesthetic authority of the Royal Academy were generally acknowledged, even by its supporters and even while it maintained considerable influence over artistic training and status. The attenuated, decadent style of James McNeill Whistler, and his famously flamboyant artistic persona, flew in the face of established taste, while John Singer Sargent's technically ambitious paintings provided a powerfully glamorous imagery of a cosmopolitan high society. The sturdy academicism of J.W. Waterhouse, Frederic, Lord Leighton, and Harry Bates evoked the art of the past while also manifesting a dedicated study of the human figure that challenged some of the core assumptions of traditional art. Although the very term 'Victorian' became a byword for old-fashioned stuffiness even before Queen Victoria was dead (1901), historians and critics have been able to explore how artists like Leighton and Waterhouse engaged with modern themes concerning the body, sexuality and the identity of the artist in complex and challenging ways.

Yet such artists provided an easy target for those who identified self-consciously with the progressive art emanating from France and Germany in the first years of the twentieth century. The pioneering efforts of Roger Fry to introduce Post-Impressionist art into Britain with his writings and exhibitions of the 1900s were matched by technically daring and visually confrontational works by Walter Richard Sickert and Duncan Grant. In a brief period of heady, pluralistic experimentation in the 1910s a multitude of styles and approaches could be seen among contemporary British artists in commercial galleries and privately organised artists' societies, and won the support of a small

Lucian Freud
Girl with a White Dog 1950–1
Oil on canvas
76.2 x 101.6
Tate. Purchased 1952

number of patrons who identified with their endeavours. Far from being simply entrenched in tradition, as has often been assumed, British artists in the first two decades of the twentieth century were among the most forward-looking in Europe. Jacob Epstein and Wyndham Lewis pursued the most abrasive kinds of modern images, which through their fragmentation and multiplicity were meant to evoke the disconcerting violence of contemporary life.

The Great War of 1914–18 can be singled out as a vastly traumatic turning point in British history. In the visual arts the war marked a general desire for a return to order, and a growing sense of nostalgia and even conservatism, which have seemed to cast a long shadow over British cultural life. The question, as poet, critic and champion of modern art Herbert Read put it in the 1930s, was 'Why the English have no Taste' – why, that is, the national 'condition' dictated 'an immense indifference to questions of art'. Modernist art and design had, in fact, a much greater presence in British culture than has perhaps hitherto been acknowledged. Yet the modern artists acclaimed by critics like Read – Henry Moore, Barbara Hepworth and Ben Nicholson prominent among them – could appear an embattled crew, isolated from popular taste and the dominant art institutions, sustained by a few highbrow critics and privileged patrons, and all too quickly lampooned in the general press. Infamously, such a view was given a very public airing when in 1949 the BBC broadcast the (reputedly booze-fuelled) speech of the outgoing President of the Academy, Sir Alfred Munnings, who violently denounced modern art and spoke up for a defiant kind of British common sense. Alternatively, there were recurring arguments for a specifically national adaptation of modernist ideals, which claimed that the abstraction and technical experimentation associated with Continental art could be combined with an intense, even visionary, focus on natural forms inherited from nineteenth-century artists like Blake and Palmer – a tendency exemplified in the works of Graham Sutherland and Paul Nash. The persistent presence of figurative painters, from Stanley Spencer and Edward Burra to Francis Bacon and Lucian Freud, alongside efforts by Ben Nicholson and Victor Pasmore, and, in sculpture, Anthony Caro and Philip King, to pursue stringent forms of abstraction, are testament to a highly diversified market for art, and a diffuse and varied system of art school training.

Although artists had at various points quite deliberately formed themselves into groups and exhibiting societies, the overall range of techniques and approaches in British art during the first half of the twentieth century was already considerable, and only grew in pace and scope in the period following the Second World War. From the pioneering and epic abstract landscapes of Peter Lanyon, through the challenging artistic and philosophical activities of John Latham, to the engaging figurative paintings of David Hockney, British art of the 1960s and 1970s appears wildly diverse, responding to a multi-faceted and rapidly changing cultural scene, the growing dominance of American culture and the mass media, and the perceived, disorientating movement from affluence and opportunity to bitter political divisions and threatened social decay.

Delineating the historical forces and social influences that have shaped the art of the last thirty years is a task best left to future historians. The even greater multiplicity and variety in the ideas and techniques of contemporary art defy easy generalisation and have gone beyond the rubric of Postmodernism, which temporarily offered a way of theorising and making sense of such variety as a comment on the fragmented nature of contemporary life. The by now rather infamous labelling in the 1990s of a generation of artists, including Sarah Lucas and Damien Hirst, as 'YBAs' (Young British Artists) may have made a contribution to the 're-branding' of Britain as fresh and cool and energetic but perhaps rather less to the understanding of the individual achievements of these figures, and less still to the historical understanding of their art in relation either to the sculptural work of the slightly older generation who came to the fore in the 1980s, or even to the work of some of the conceptual artists of the 1970s. British artists since the 1990s have operated in a truly global context, developing a highly differentiated range of practices and complex ways of engaging with the world. Whatever the reality of the situation, for a period it has seemed that the old antagonism towards the modern that supposedly marked British life has been overturned, and the potential for artists to become celebrities has become a reality as never before.

Art of the present day may call into question the relationship between the gallery and the world, emphasising the artifice and illusion involved in the spaces where it is made and presented, and raising difficult questions about the complicity of artists and their spectators. As regards the national collection of British art, these contemporary critical questions about art and its contexts take on a highly significant historical dimension. The rather airy philosophical problems of defining 'art' and its values are preceded in this respect by some much more prosaic issues. Tate's Collection operates around established historical boundaries developed over the century or so of its history; it collects, displays and interprets British art from around 1500 to the present day and international art of the twentieth and now twenty-first centuries. This starting date for the Collection implies a whole range of assumptions about the nature and techniques of art and the identity of the artist. Implicitly, the Collection ranges over the period subsequent to the arrival in Britain of Hans Holbein and, with him, of the Renaissance concept of the individual artist creating unique works for elite patrons. The unnamed artists of the Middle Ages or earlier are not considered within the Collection; the decorative arts, architecture and even sculpture are excluded, for Tate's Collection of sculpture officially begins only with works by artists who were contemporary at the foundation of the gallery. The representation of historic works on paper was bolstered by the acquisition of a large number from the collection of Paul Oppé in 1996, but while landscape watercolours from the late eighteenth and nineteenth centuries are now relatively well represented, the art of caricature – widely considered as a highly significant facet of visual culture in the eighteenth and nineteenth centuries – is barely present. Pre-twentieth-century Scottish and Irish artists are generally thinly represented, except in the cases of artists (like James Barry or David Wilkie) who made their name in London. Works by amateur artists from the past, which have become recognised over recent years as an important component in the history of art, are relatively few in number. The whole realm of 'folk arts', 'popular culture' and artisan productions – a realm whose definition is an immensely fraught matter in itself, encompassing everything from genteel pastimes to ships' figureheads – is also beyond the remit of the national collection. Yet its importance as a context for and point of reference within fine art practice has been increasingly recognised among artists, historians and critics.

So, despite its evident, indeed unparalleled, richness, the national collection of British art showcased at Tate Britain is marked by certain omissions and restrictions. These can be, and are, addressed through strategic acquisitions, through loans and exhibitions, and through new research and publications. Foreign-born artists have been brought into the Collection in greater numbers than in the past, and amateur artists find a place that they lacked before. The further challenge of matching Tate's representation of Britain and British art to the historical and contemporary realities of national life is pressing and considerable. The hundred works presented here reveal British art's historical and contemporary richness. The presence of artists of different cultural backgrounds is evidence of the diversity of British culture in the past and the present, and the range of techniques, moods and styles exhibited here testifies to the great variety of different interests that artists have addressed

Mark Wallinger
State Britain 2007
Mixed media
40 metres
Installation, courtesy the artist

over time and in different contexts. However, we should be wary of treating the national collection as a kind of 'Noah's Ark' of British culture where eventually, if enough additions or extensions are made to the scope of the Collection on a short-term or permanent basis, the totality of British art – and perhaps Britain itself – will somehow be represented. It may be, rather, that the provisionality and open-endedness of our concept of British art are more productive, connecting and reconnecting the past and the present, the individual and the collective in many, various and sometimes awkward or uncomfortable ways.

John Bettes
(active 1531–1570)

A Man in a Black Cap 1545
Oil on oak panel
47 x 41
Purchased 1897

This is the earliest picture in the Tate Collection and is painted on wooden panel. The artist's name and nationality – English – are inscribed on the back. The various inscriptions visible on the front indicate that the work was painted 'in the year of Our Lord 1545' and that the sitter was aged twenty-six.

John Bettes is first recorded carrying out decorative work for King Henry VIII's court in 1531–3, and he may have worked with the German incomer artist Hans Holbein II (1497/8–1543). This portrait was originally larger and would have had a blue background similar to the colour often used by Holbein. Due mainly to long exposure to light, the principal pigment (called 'smalt') has changed hue from blue to brown.

Marcus Gheeraerts II
(1561/2–1636)

Portrait of an Unknown Lady c.1595
Oil on wood
92.7 x 76
Accepted by H.M. Government in lieu
of tax and allocated to the Tate Gallery
2001

Recent research has established that a number of Elizabethan and Jacobean portraits (from c.1562 to c.1630) unmistakably show women in an advanced state of pregnancy. This seems to be an unusual phenomenon in Western art, and may have arisen through specific dynastic concerns, combined with anxiety about possible death in childbirth.

The Flemish-born, but London-raised, painter Marcus Gheeraerts II is well represented in the Tate Collection. He produced various such 'pregnancy portraits', and Tate acquired this example in 2001. Although the identity of the sitter is unknown, her sumptuous costume, adorned with numerous pearls of varying sizes, indicates her high status. Pearls also symbolised purity, an appropriate allusion to a chaste wife. It is unusual for a sitter of this period to be shown smiling, as here, but this feature is found also in other portraits by Gheeraerts.

Anon, British School
(17th century)

The Cholmondeley Ladies c.1600–10
Oil on wood
88.6 x 172.3
Presented anonymously 1955

According to the inscription on this painting (bottom left), it shows 'Two Ladies of the Cholmondeley Family, Who were born the same day, Married the same day, And brought to Bed [gave birth] the same day.' To mark this dynastic event, they are formally presented in bed, their babies wrapped in high-status scarlet fabric.

Although at a superficial glance they appear identical, in fact the lace, jewellery and eye colours of the ladies and infants are carefully differentiated. The side-by-side, half-length, head-on format echoes tomb sculpture of the period. The ladies, whose precise identities are unclear, were probably painted by an artist based in the city of Chester, near the Cholmondeley family estates.

David des Granges
(c.1611–?1675)

The Saltonstall Family c.1640
Oil on canvas
214 x 276.2
Purchased with assistance from the
Friends of the Tate Gallery, The Art Fund
and the Pilgrim Trust 1976

This great family piece is something of a puzzle. It apparently takes its inspiration from the elaborate dynastic tombs of the period, on which the living and the dead are shown intermingled. What we think is being shown is Sir Richard Saltonstall (1595–1650), of Chipping Warden, Oxfordshire, drawing back the red curtain round the bed that contains his deceased first wife, who gestures towards the couple's two surviving children, Richard and Ann. He, meanwhile, gazes towards his second – living – wife, who sits holding her own Saltonstall baby, tightly swaddled. As was usual at this period, the younger Richard wears a long

skirt – boys only adopted breeches at around the age of seven. Both ladies wear costly lace. The red hangings of the bed demonstrate wealth and high status, and to the left and right can be seen the edges of a richly patterned tapestry, echoing those woven at Mortlake, near London. Almost every area of the canvas resonates with pattern and colour.

David des Granges, who is traditionally said to have painted this picture, was principally a miniaturist, later working for King Charles II. Of French incomer origin, he was baptised in London in 1611.

Francis Cleyn
(c.1582–1658)

Samuel's Reproach to Saul c.1630–5
Pencil, pen and ink and wash on paper
24.5 x 39.6
Purchased 1990

Born in Rostock, in the Duchy of Mecklenburg-Schwerin on the Baltic coast, in what is now Germany, Cleyn (or Clein) pursued an international career. Probably trained in the Netherlands, he travelled in Italy and by 1617 was in Copenhagen, working at the Danish court. From 1625 Cleyn was in England, employed principally as the chief designer at the Mortlake tapestry works. An expensive commodity, tapestry was an essential component of European court splendour and the Mortlake factory was sponsored by the crown.

Surviving designs by Cleyn are rare, but it is not clear if this is a design for a tapestry or for a print (Cleyn produced print series and book illustrations, particularly in the latter part of his career). A biblical scene, it shows Saul being reproached by Samuel following the war against the Amalekites. Commanded by God to spare no one, Saul had in fact captured the Amalekite king (who can be seen in the background) as well as the best livestock (a flock of sheep is further down the hill). Saul grabbed and tore off a piece of Samuel's robe, which prompted Samuel to say that God would tear the kingdom of Israel from Saul.

William Dobson
(1611–1646)

Endymion Porter c.1642–5
Oil on canvas
149.9 x 127
Purchased 1888

Endymion Porter (1587–1649), a courtier of King Charles I, was knowledgeable about art – a useful skill at Charles I's court. He is depicted here as a huntsman with a wheel-lock sporting rifle and attended by an awed-looking page and dog, around the beginning of the Civil War in Britain. Porter's interests are indicated by the half-length statue of Apollo (upper left), patron god of the arts, and by the frieze that he leans against, which is carved with figures representing the arts.

William Dobson probably painted this portrait at Charles I's court in Oxford, as Porter was a member of the exiled parliament there. The pose is borrowed from a sixteenth-century painting by Titian of the Roman Emperor Vespasian, which was then in Charles I's collection. Porter was later forced into exile on the Continent, and his own art collection – of which no details are known – was dispersed.

Nathaniel Bacon
(1585–1627)

Cookmaid with Still Life of
Vegetables and Fruit c.1620–25
Oil on canvas
151 x 246.7
Purchased with assistance from
The Art Fund 1995

Sir Nathaniel Bacon was of higher social status than other English-born artists, and painted for his own interest rather than for money. Although he was outstandingly talented, very few works attributable to him survive today.

The present subject matter, a kitchen maid seated within an exuberant display of produce, is generally associated with Dutch or Flemish painting. The only English artist known to have painted such works is Bacon, and it is likely that he received some training in the Low Countries. Each item depicted seems to have been grown in England at this time. Bacon himself raised melons on his estate at Brome in Suffolk.

Jan Siberechts
(1627–c.1700)

**View of a House and its
Estate in Belsize, Middlesex** 1696
Oil on canvas
107.9 x 139.7
Purchased with assistance from The Art
Fund and the Friends of the Tate Gallery
1995

This painting is effectively a portrait of a house and its surrounding gardens and grounds. Offering a bird's-eye view, it presents the estate as productive and well ordered. It is thought that in 1696, the date on this work, the property belonged to a successful goldsmith and banker called John Coggs. Belsize today is part of north-west London, but at this date it was a distant rural retreat for affluent middle-class inhabitants of the City of London. When the painting was made, the overall landlord of the whole area of Belsize was the Dean and Chapter of Westminster Abbey – and the abbey can just be seen on the horizon here.

The Flemish artist Jan Siberechts settled in Britain in the early 1670s and began to specialise in producing paintings of estates. He evidently travelled the length of England for this purpose, and most estates that he pictured were grander than this comparatively modest residence.

Philip Mercier
(?1689–1760)

**The Schutz Family and their
Friends on a Terrace** 1725
Oil on canvas
102.2 x 125.7
Purchased 1980

Born and trained in Berlin, Mercier arrived in England in 1715. He is closely identified with the development of the conversation piece – a type of small-scale group portrait showing friends and families in private, relaxed and at ease. Their genteel informality reflects the cultural shift in the early eighteenth century from the rigid grandeur of the previous age. Although the genre has Dutch and Flemish origins, Mercier's delicate style was influenced by the work of Antoine Watteau (1684–1721), with which he had become familiar when in France and after which he made etchings.

This elegant outdoor gathering, with card games being played on an imposing garden terrace, possibly shows members of the Schutz family, who, like many of Mercier's early patrons in England, were closely connected with the Hanoverian court. It is most likely a wedding portrait, the central couple being Augustus Schutz, future Keeper of the Privy Purse and Master of the Robes to George II, and his bride Penelope, in pink with flowers in her hair, Lady in Waiting to Queen Caroline. It has been argued that the horse in the background is the white horse of Saxony, emblem of the House of Hanover, a symbol of the family's allegiance to the Hanoverian succession.

Francis Hayman
(1708–1776)

**Samuel Richardson, the Novelist
(1684–1761), Seated, Surrounded
by his Second Family** 1740–1
Oil on canvas
99.5 x 125.2
Purchased with assistance from the
National Heritage Memorial Fund,
The Art Fund and Tate Members 2006

Francis Hayman was a portraitist, history painter and genre painter, and one of the leading lights in the artistic community of London in the first half of the eighteenth century. A close friend of William Hogarth, he was also a major influence on the young Thomas Gainsborough, who arrived in London at precisely the time when the present portrait was painted.

This portrait is among Hayman's finest works. The importance of the painting lies also in the significance of the subject to British cultural life, being a portrait of the novelist Samuel Richardson with his second wife and young family; Richardson's first marriage had ended in tragedy with the death of his wife and all of his six children. In the autumn of 1740 Richardson achieved overnight success with the publication of his first novel, *Pamela or Virtue Rewarded*, a seminal work in the history of English literature. The book, which charts the trials and tribulations of an innocent serving maid in defence of her virtue, went through five editions in its first year. The sixth edition, published in 1742, was illustrated with twenty-nine plates by Hayman, which were engraved by the French artist, Hubert Gravelot. This portrait by Hayman was probably made towards the end of 1740, just after the book's publication, and may have been conceived to celebrate Richardson's success.

John Vanderbank
(1694–1739)

Equestrian Design: The Volte Renversée to the Right 1728
Pencil and watercolour on paper
25.7 x 17.4
Purchased as part of the Oppé Collection with assistance from the National Lottery through the Heritage Lottery Fund 1996

This sketch, in pencil and grey wash, relates to the publication *Twenty Five Actions of the Manage Horse*, a manual on horsemanship and dressage published by Joseph Sympson and Andrew Johnston in 1729. The illustrative plates were engraved by Sympson after drawings by Vanderbank. This drawing appears, in reverse, as plate 12: 'The Volte renversee to the right, when a horse moves with his head to the centre & hind quarters without the Volte, the best lesson to make a horses shoulders pliable'.

Although better known as a portraitist, Vanderbank was also a skilled draughtsman. In 1720, in partnership with the decorative artist Louis Chéron, he had founded the St Martin's Lane Academy, an artist's academy that promoted observational life drawing. In the introduction to *Twenty Five Actions of the Manage Horse* Sympson tells us that, 'to better execute his ideas, [Vanderbank] was himself a Disciple in our Riding-Schools, and purchased a fine Horse as a Model for his Pencil'. Vanderbank worked for print publishers in the latter part of his career presumably through financial necessity (in 1729 he suffered a spell in Marshalsea prison for debt). He also produced repeats of his equestrian designs for clients, capitalising on the original success of the book.

Andrea Soldi
(c.1703–1771)

Portrait of Henry Lannoy Hunter in Oriental Dress, Resting from Hunting, with a Manservant Holding Game c.1733–6
Oil on canvas
118.5 x 146
Purchased with assistance from
Tate patrons and The Art Fund 2004

Before settling in England, where he quickly became established as a successful society portraitist, the Italian artist Soldi travelled in the eastern Mediterranean. In the mid-1730s he was in Aleppo where, according to the eighteenth-century antiquary George Vertue, he 'became acquainted with some English Merchants whose pictures having drawn with approbation they advised him to come to England which he did'. Aleppo was the trading capital of Syria, then under Ottoman rule, and was the location for the English Levant Company's most important factory. The Hunter family's extensive Levant trade sustained their profession as London dyers, and Henry Lannoy Hunter served his

merchant apprenticeship at Aleppo, before returning to England in 1733. He is shown in elaborate Turkish attire, seated on an oriental rug, the embodiment of the wealthy company merchant, while about him are trophies of the day's hunting (a frequent pastime of Aleppo merchants). The distant coastline could well be the bay of 'Scanderoon' (Iskenderun), the port that served Aleppo, a panoramic view of which could be had from the Bylan mountains, where British merchants escaped the summer heat. The portrait was painted either in Aleppo or shortly after Soldi's arrival in England, as a result of contacts forged in the Near East.

James Thornhill
(1675/6–1734)

**Design for Invitation Card for the
Feast of St Luke** 1718
Pencil, chalk, pen and ink, brush and ink
and ink wash on paper
18.7 x 30.5
Purchased as part of the Oppé Collection
with assistance from the National Lottery
through the Heritage Lottery Fund 1996

The Virtuosi of St Luke was the oldest
and most prestigious art club in England.
Its members were prominent artists and
patrons who met once a week (once a
month in summer) at a London tavern to
discuss art and connoisseurship. Each year
the elected club steward presided over
the annual celebration of St Luke, patron
saint of artists. A splendid dinner of
'Westfallen ham' would be followed by a
picture raffle and a discussion of the work's
aesthetic merits.

In 1718 the baroque decorative painter
James Thornhill was the club's steward.
An eminent figure in the London art world,
in the same year he had been appointed
the king's history painter and he was also
governor of the important Great Queen
Street Academy. His design for the invitation
card for the Virtuosi's feast incorporates an
oval canvas with St Luke painting the
Madonna and Child. A bacchic satyr alludes
to the expected conviviality of the occasion
and symbols of the arts surround the
scrolled paper inviting members and guests.
In the background is St Paul's Church,
Covent Garden, a reference to the location
of the feast (at Thornhill's house on the
Piazza), as well as to Covent Garden as the
heart of the artistic community.

William Hogarth
(1697–1764)

The Painter and his Pug 1745
Oil on canvas
90 x 69.9
Purchased 1824

Hogarth first began this celebrated self-portrait in the mid-1730s. X-rays have revealed that at this stage it showed the artist in a formal coat and wig. Later, however, he introduced the more informal cap and clothes seen here. Developed over several years, the portrait is also Hogarth's public statement of his artistic beliefs. It represents the artist in a still-life assemblage as if painted on an unframed oval canvas, which rests on the volumes of the three authors that he admired most: Shakespeare, Swift and Milton. The implication is not only that he took his inspiration from drama, contemporary satire and epic poetry but also that he saw the art of painting as their equal. In the left foreground lies his palette bearing the representation of the three-dimensional, serpentine 'Line of Beauty and Grace', which Hogarth considered to be the fundamental principle of all artistic harmony and beauty. In the opposite corner, as if to contrast the reality of nature with theoretical abstraction, sits one of Hogarth's successive favourite pugs. In this case it is probably Trump, whose features resemble his own. Indeed, Hogarth was fond of remarking on the resemblance between himself and his dog and probably saw in it something suggestive of his own notoriously pugnacious character.

Allan Ramsay
(1713–1784)

**Thomas, 2nd Baron Mansel of Margam
with his Blackwood Half-Brothers
and Sister** 1742
Oil on canvas
124.5 x 100.3
Purchased with assistance from the
National Heritage Memorial Fund, the
National Art Collections Fund (Woodroffe
Bequest), the Friends of the Tate Gallery,
the Mail on Sunday through the Friends
of the Tate Gallery, Arthur Young,
Mrs Sue Hammerson and others 1988

This picture is unusual for Ramsay, as he
rarely painted sentimental or affectionate
group portraits. It shows Thomas, 2nd
Baron Mansel of Margam, Glamorgan, who
was then in his early twenties. Mansel's
mother, the daughter of the celebrated
admiral, Sir Cloudesley Shovel, had first
married the Hon. Robert Mansel. On his
death she married John Blackwood of
Charlton, Kent, and produced three
children, Shovel, Mary and John.

In the painting Thomas Mansel stands at
the right, holding his gun and the partridge
he has just shot. At his side stand his eldest
half-brother, Shovel, and Mary, who rests
her hand on the bird's breast. The youngest
child, John, is seated at the left, smiling
towards the viewer. In Ramsay's picture, an
early visual image of eighteenth-century
sensibility, Thomas looks down tenderly at
his half-sister Mary, who is visually impaired.
Perhaps in order to demonstrate the
importance to her of the sense of touch, she
places her hand over the bird; the distinctive
reddy-brown horseshoe mark on the
partridge's breast is part of its natural
plumage, although it looks like blood. The
painting was probably commissioned to
commemorate the children's mother, who
had died in 1741.

Thomas Gainsborough
(1727–1788)

**Peter Darnell Muilman, Charles Crokatt
and William Keable in a Landscape** c.1750
Oil on canvas
76.5 x 64.2
Purchased jointly with Gainsborough's
House, Sudbury, with assistance from
the National Heritage Memorial Fund,
the National Art Collections Fund and the
Friends of the Tate Gallery 1993

Gainsborough's intimate portrait of three
young men in a landscape is one of his
most striking and enchanting early
paintings. As with his other similar works
of this period, the carefully delineated
naturalistic landscape background reflects
Gainsborough's love of his native Suffolk,
with its rutted roads, oak coppices and
open skies. The three men in the picture
have been identified as (from left to right)
Charles Crokatt, William Keable and Peter
Darnell Muilman. The picture was
commissioned by Muilman's father Henry, a
prosperous London merchant, a commission
probably instigated by the move to East
Anglia of the Muilman and Crokatt families
in 1749. As they had acquired estates in
Essex at this very time, the picture can be
viewed as a propaganda exercise relating
to their acceptance into the local landed
gentry. Henry Muilman may also have
wanted a portrait of his own son with his
future son-in-law, for his daughter was to
marry Charles Crokatt in April 1752. Keable,
the figure at the centre of the composition,
was, like Gainsborough, a portrait painter
and an amateur musician. His role here as
flautist suggests that he served Crokatt and
Muilman as a music master, and may also
have taught them drawing.

Johan Zoffany
(1733–1810)

Three Sons of John, 3rd Earl of Bute

c.1763–4
Oil on canvas
100.9 x 126
Accepted by H.M. Government in lieu of tax with additional payment (General Funds) made with assistance from the National Lottery through the Heritage Lottery Fund, the National Art Collections Fund and Tate Members 2002

Johan Zoffany was born in Germany and trained there and in Italy before arriving in England in 1760. Although his earlier work comprised principally religious and mythological paintings, Zoffany quickly adapted to his new environment, and his small-scale, informal, group portraits, or 'conversation pieces', established him as the leading artist of the genre in London.

This work is one of a lively pair of portraits commissioned by John Stuart, 3rd Earl of Bute, one of Zoffany's first important British patrons. Lord Bute was then George III's favoured prime minister although he resigned from that position in 1763 at around the time of this commission.

Bute probably introduced Zoffany to the king and queen, commencing a highly successful period of royal patronage for the artist. In the present portrait Bute's three younger sons have temporarily abandoned their game of archery to go bird-nesting, the boy in the tree holding in his right hand a young goldfinch. In the pendant picture (not illustrated here) Bute's three daughters are depicted playing with pet squirrels. The setting for both portraits is Bute's country estate, Luton Park, Bedfordshire, which he acquired in 1763. Zoffany's portraits therefore displayed simultaneously Bute's progeny and his status as an important magnate and landowner.

THE ARCHBISHOP of ARMAGH AND BROTHERS WHEN BOYS.

Joshua Reynolds
(1723–1792)

Colonel Acland and Lord Sydney:
The Archers 1769
Oil on canvas
236 x 180
Purchased (Building the Tate Collection fund)
with assistance from the National Heritage
Memorial Fund, Tate Members, The Art Fund
(with a contribution from the Wolfson
Foundation) and other donors 2005

This full-length double portrait is among
the most important and visually impressive
portraits by Joshua Reynolds, who was
himself one of the leading artists in
eighteenth-century Europe by virtue of his
portraiture, his presidency of the Royal
Academy of Arts and his authorship of the
Discourses on Art. When Reynolds exhibited
this painting at the Royal Academy in 1770,
he entitled it 'The portraits of two
gentlemen: whole lengths'. Since then it
has become better known simply as
The Archers.

The picture depicts two young aristocrats,
Dudley Alexander Sydney Cosby, Lord
Sydney (1732–74), shown on the left, and

Colonel John Dyke Acland (1746–78). Colonel
Acland was a politician and soldier who
fought in the war against the American
colonists, while Lord Sydney pursued a
diplomatic career until his death by suicide
in 1774. In *The Archers* Reynolds drew
particularly on the visual language of Titian's
late *poesie*, or mythological subjects,
notably his great composition, *The Death
of Actaeon* (National Gallery, London). The
portrait also recalls the tradition of grand
baroque hunting scenes, while the pile of
dead game is modelled on a still-life painting
by the Flemish animal and still-life painter,
Frans Snyders, which at the time belonged
to Reynolds's friend, Dr William Hunter.

Richard Wilson
(1713–1782)

Llyn-y-Cau, Cader Idris ?exhibited 1774
Oil on canvas
51.1 x 73
Presented by Sir Edward Marsh 1945

Lyn-y-Cau is a volcanic lake, near the top of Cader Idris mountain in Merionethshire, North Wales. To the left is the valley of the Dysynni, bordered by the cliffs of Craig Goch, while the Bay of Cardigan lies in the distance. Wilson has rendered the view in an extremely summary fashion: the foreground is entirely imaginary, while the contours of the central crag are nowhere as regular or as elevated as they appear here. These and other departures from topographical fact enabled Wilson to wrest a perceptible sense of order from an inherently chaotic scene.

In this picture, as in his other Welsh landscapes, Wilson presents Wales as a paradise of primitive simplicity, to where people can retreat from the confusions of the modern world and contemplate the natural and divinely ordained rhythms of life. Though the site was hardly a famous one at the time when he painted it – and he was probably the first artist ever to have done so – Wilson's vision of ordered wildness appears to have found several willing buyers. One reason for its appeal may have been that the view, although set in Wales, was reminiscent of the volcanic lakes, particularly around Naples, that were popular attractions on the Grand Tourist trail.

Thomas Jones
(1742–1803)

**An Excavation of an Antique Building
in a Cava in the Villa Negroni, Rome**
?1777, later dated 1779
Oil and chalk on paper
40.6 x 55.2
Presented by Canon J.H. Adams 1983

This is one of the few known depictions of an excavation made in Rome during the eighteenth century, which is surprising, since it was such a commonplace activity at that time. Jones evidently painted this scene (or at least made the crayon underdrawing of it) on or shortly after 5 July 1777, the date recorded in his 'Memoirs' for his visit to the newly discovered site. There he wrote: 'went with Tresham to see the Antique Rooms just discovered, by digging for antient Bricks, in the Villa Negroni – The painted Ornaments much in the Chinese taste – figures of Cupids bathing &c and painted in *fresco* on the Stucco of the Walls – The Reds, purples, Blues & Yellows very bright – but had a dark & heavy effect – NB Tresham made a purchase of these paintings for 50 Crowns, to be taken off the walls at his Own Expence –'

Jones probably gained access to the excavation site, which was a lucrative source of income for traders in antique artefacts, through the dealer Thomas Jenkins, who had been a friend of Jones's teacher Richard Wilson in Rome during the 1750s. Henry Tresham, an artist as well as an art dealer, apparently made a handsome profit on the Villa Negroni frescoes, which he sold to the Earl-Bishop of Derry.

Joseph Wright of Derby
(1737–1797)

An Iron Forge 1772
Oil on canvas
121.3 x 132
Purchased with assistance from the
National Heritage Memorial Fund,
The Art Fund and the Friends of the
Tate Gallery 1992

Joseph Wright was a portrait- and subject-painter based in Derby, Liverpool and London. He is now best remembered for his scenes of contemporary industrial and scientific life. This picture shows a small iron forge at work, with what we must assume is the forge-master's extended family looking on. Although the painting is often taken as an illustration of the Industrial Revolution, the technology that Wright depicts was not especially advanced. Rather, the modernity of the painting lies in its heroic treatment of a theme from common life. The extraordinary light effects and dramatic composition endow this everyday scene of working men with almost religious grandeur, and by showing the various members of the family, Wright may be hinting at the noble theme of the 'ages of man'. According to high-minded art theories promoted by the elite classes, such a prosaic scene from the life of ordinary working people did not deserve such a dignified treatment. Through the mass publication of prints after his works, and the public exhibition of his paintings, Wright reached out to new and less exclusive audiences for art.

George Stubbs
(1724–1806)

Reapers 1785
Oil on wood
89.9 x 136.8
Purchased with assistance from the Friends of the Tate Gallery, The Art Fund, the Pilgrim Trust and subscribers 1977

This is one of a pair of pictures by Stubbs showing rural labour. The other picture, featuring haymakers, is also in the Tate Collection. Stubbs showed this pair of pictures at the annual exhibition of the Royal Academy in 1786. He must have hoped to capitalise on the established taste for sentimental rural scenes. However, the pictures were generally not well received. Stubbs's reputation was for painting precise scenes of horses and sporting life, and critics did not warm to this change of direction.

Arguably, Stubbs's picture presents a greatly idealised view of rural life: the workers are spotlessly clean despite their drudgery, and the women are dressed in up-to-date fashions. The church in the far distance to the left and the farm manager on the horse to the right may serve as reminders of spiritual and social authority. Thus the picture can be seen as a celebration of the order and nobility of rural life, in tune with the concern for efficiency shown by agricultural writers of the time like Arthur Young. Alternatively, it may be said to rob these labourers of their individuality and to deny the harsh realities of work for sentimental effect.

John Singleton Copley
(1738–1815)

The Death of Major Peirson, 6 January 1781
1783
Oil on canvas
251.5 x 365.8
Purchased 1864

This large painting depicts a battle between French and English troops that took place on Jersey in 1781 during a conflict sparked off by French support for the American War of Independence. During the skirmish the young Major Peirson was killed, and his black servant immediately avenged his death. Following the lead of his mentor and fellow American, Benjamin West, Copley became famous for painting dramatic scenes of contemporary events in an elevated pictorial style. Here the composition as a whole refers to a tradition of painting scenes from history or the Bible; the group around Peirson recalls depictions of Christ's descent from the Cross, while the women and children on the right derive from a painting by Raphael. In painting a contemporary news event, Copley was appealing to a wider audience than that familiar with more traditional subject matter. The painting was put on public show, not at the official exhibition of the Royal Academy but at a privately rented venue where visitors were charged for entry. This was a novel sort of display and marked the emergence of art as a kind of urban spectacle or entertainment, rather than being the private pleasure of only the wealthiest.

Johan Zoffany
(1733–1810)

Colonel Mordaunt's Cock Match c.1784–6
Oil on canvas
113.5 x 149.8
Purchased with assistance from the
National Heritage Memorial Fund,
The Art Fund, the Friends of the Tate Gallery
and a group of donors 1994

This picture shows a cock match in India, at the court of Asaf-ud-Daula, Nawab Wazir of Oudh. A fight is starting between the Nawab's cock and one of Colonel John Mordaunt's prizefighters imported from England. Mordaunt, an English mercenary who was commander of the Nawab's bodyguard, is shown standing to the left in white. Many of the other figures are identifiable, including the artist, who is seated at the top right.

The lifestyle of Westerners in India was notorious for its immorality and corruption. Great fortunes were made there by businessmen and soldiers, who often came from outside Britain's ruling elite, and the geographical distance from Britain meant that social rules were relaxed. Cockfighting itself was frowned upon at home. In Zoffany's painting the unconventionality of colonial life in India is expressed in the most rowdy terms. The Nawab appears to be shown aroused, and within the general chaos of the scene figures embrace and interact in suggestive ways. However, the picture was commissioned by Warren Hastings, the Governor-General of Bengal, and it seems unlikely that the picture was meant to be simply critical of colonial life.

James Barry
(1741–1806)

**King Lear Weeping over the
Dead Body of Cordelia** 1786–8
Oil on canvas
269.2 x 367
Purchased 1962

The subject of this painting is taken from the conclusion of Shakespeare's play *King Lear* (c.1603–6). The ancient British King Lear is shown mad with grief, holding up the body of his youngest daughter Cordelia. His vanity and bad judgement have led to discord in the nation, terrible wars, plots and assassinations, and ultimately to Cordelia's tragic murder, which drives him to suicide. The brutal ending of Shakespeare's play had always been changed in eighteenth-century stage productions, to suit the more sentimental tastes of the times. Barry's painting emphasises instead a sense of primitive grandeur and emotional violence. It thus reflects the new taste for shocking and sensational subjects, associated with the aesthetic category of the Sublime.

Barry's huge painting was created for the print publisher John Boydell. In 1786 he had announced plans for a 'Shakespeare Gallery'. This would feature newly commissioned paintings of Shakespearean subjects executed by leading painters. The gallery first opened in 1789 and encouraged a number of similar schemes involving paintings based on poetic and historical subjects. These provided an important stimulus for British painters and helped consolidate a growing sense of national pride focused on the literary heritage.

Thomas Lawrence
(1769–1830)

Mrs Siddons 1804
Oil on canvas
254 x 148
Presented by Mrs C. Fitzhugh 1843

Brought up in hardship in the country, the son of a debt-ridden innkeeper, Lawrence was virtually self-taught but became the most brilliant and fashionable portrait-painter of his generation. His reputation was known across Europe, where his work was thought to exemplify a typically English way of painting – spontaneous, expressive and utterly assured. He painted a glittering aristocracy at the height of its confidence and privilege, but also the intellectual elite, whom he endowed with equal if not greater *gravitas*.

Sophia Siddons was the supreme Shakespearean actress of her day. By the time this portrait was painted, she was nearing the climax of her career; she retired in 1812. Rather than appearing on the stage in one of her classic roles, such as Lady Macbeth, she is shown giving one of the dramatic readings that she presented at court before the king and queen. She is holding open a large volume, with a smaller book of plays by Thomas Otway beside her as well as a folio entitled 'Shakespeare'.

William Blake
(1757–1827)

Elohim Creating Adam 1795/c.1805
Colour print finished in black ink and
watercolour
43.1 x 53.6
Presented by W. Graham Robertson 1939

Elohim Creating Adam is one in a cycle of twelve designs produced with a new colour-printing technique that Blake started using in 1795. Their innovatory nature is evidence of Blake seeking much longed-for public recognition – which never came.

'Elohim' is Hebrew for God. Blake emphasises the Hebrew origins of the Old Testament account in Genesis of the creation of Adam, the first man. This was the work of God, but images of this God as winged are rare. In Hebrew scripture Elohim is the ancient deity who dictates the rules that man must follow. Blake believed that these laws of organised religion, like the Ten Commandments, repressed man's imagination. But Elohim also means 'Gods'.

Through John Milton's poem *Paradise Lost* Blake knew an image of the plurality of the Christian God as the Creator: God the Father sends his Son to start the six days of creation. With his 'brooding wings … outspread' – like the descending dove symbolising the all-loving Holy Ghost – Blake changed the creating 'Spirit of God' (his Son) into a threatening presence. He is like the God of Reason, Urizen, in Blake's own mythology. Adam is rooted in the 'dust of the ground' from which God is forming him. A constraining worm grows out of Adam, rather as Eve was born out of his side. It symbolises man's mortality after Eve disobeyed God by eating the forbidden fruit.

Henry Fuseli
(1741–1825)

**The Shepherd's Dream,
from 'Paradise Lost'** 1786
Oil on canvas
154.3 x 215.3
Purchased 1966

This picture shows a peasant at rest, surrounded by an array of outlandish imps, fairies and elves. The subject is derived from John Milton's epic poem *Paradise Lost* (1667). Milton does not describe the peasant's dream itself, but uses it as a simile when he describes how Hell was becoming overcrowded with devils:

… So thick the airy crowd
Swarmed and were straitened; till the signal given.
Behold a wonder! They but now who seemed
In bigness to surpass Earth's giant sons
Now less than smallest dwarfs, in narrow room
Throng numberless, like that Pygmean race
Beyond the Indian mount, or fairy elves,

Whose midnight revels, by a forest side
Or fountain some belated peasant sees,
Or dreams he sees …

The Swiss-born painter Fuseli made a name for himself in the 1780s with fantastic scenes like this. The present picture was enthusiastically received by critics when it was exhibited at the Royal Academy in 1786, although many felt confused by the weirdness of its imagery. Fuseli's paintings pushed at the accepted boundaries of taste and showed that a visual artist could use literary source materials in a highly imaginative way, rather than simply painting direct illustrations of texts.

Joseph Mallord William Turner
(1775–1851)

Study for The Shipwreck c.1805
From Shipwreck (1) Sketchbook
Pen and ink and watercolour on paper
11.8 x 18.5
Bequeathed by the artist 1856

J.M.W. Turner was a giant in his time and has continued to astonish and inspire ever since. Tate owns the world's largest collection of his work – the paintings, watercolours, drawings and sketchbooks acquired from the artist's estate in 1856. It displays the extraordinary achievements of this great Romantic painter: from early topographical drawings or classical oils to spectacular late watercolours; ideal and natural landscapes; historical subjects ancient and modern; tributes to the Old Masters and works of pure originality;

marines; literary illustrations; and more.

Turner's sketchbooks are full of fascinating insights, a memory bank for his pictures, which are densely layered with meaning. Shipwrecks in an early sketchbook may have been prompted by news of actual events or by composite impressions of dangers at sea, or simply inspired by literature. In painting Hannibal assailed by tribesmen in an Alpine storm on his way to invade Italy, Turner had the contemporary invader, Napoleon, in mind. ❯❯

**Snow Storm: Hannibal and his Army
Crossing the Alps** exhibited 1812
Oil on canvas
146 x 237.5
Bequeathed by the artist 1856

Joseph Mallord William Turner
(1775–1851)

Venice: The Giudecca Canal, Looking towards Fusina at Sunset 1840
From Roll Sketchbook of Venice
Pencil, watercolour and crayon on paper
22.1 x 32.3
Bequeathed by the artist 1856

In the same way that Venice had inspired many of his finest works in both oil and watercolour, Turner made Alpine scenery his own, transformed by dazzling effects of weather and light. In late paintings like *Norham Castle, Sunrise* he modified scenes familiar from his earlier work, dissolving form and substance into atmosphere in an abstract manner that points to Impressionism and beyond.

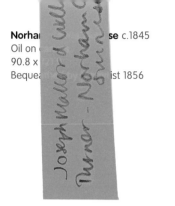

Norha **se** c.1845
Oil on
90.8 x
Beque ist 1856

John Constable
(1776–1837)

Flatford Mill ('Scene on a Navigable River')
1816–17
Oil on canvas
101.6 x 127
Bequeathed by Miss Isabel Constable
as the gift of Maria Louisa, Isabel and
Lionel Bicknell Constable 1888

John Constable was determined to transform landscape painting, raising it from an imitative art like portraiture to one capable of the highest moral and emotive powers, and based on nature more than style. He dedicated himself to 'natural painture' (painting). He never travelled abroad and found many of his most important images in the Stour valley between Suffolk and Essex, where he grew up. As he said, its scenery 'made me a painter'. His treatment of native English landscape was pioneering in its naturalism, apparent simplicity and use of studies made from nature. At first these were separate sketches, but by the time he made this picture he was experimenting with painting outdoors from nature as well.

Dating from summer 1816, this is a view of the Stour towards Flatford Mill, which belonged to his father Golding Constable, as did the barges that transported grain downstream to Mistley for shipment to London and returned with coal. Golding died in 1816 and this picture of the productive, prosperous landscape of Constable's 'careless boyhood' may be partly a memorial to him.

John Linnell
(1792–1882)

Kensington Gravel Pits 1811–12
Oil on canvas
71.1 x 106.7
Purchased 1947

Though the most persuasive, Constable was not the only naturalist painter of his generation. The watercolourist John Varley advised friends and pupils, including John Linnell, to 'Go to nature for everything' and encouraged them to draw and paint outdoors. Linnell took this advice when he was living in London near what is now Notting Hill Gate from 1809 to 1811. A contemporary remembered him 'sitting down before any common object, the paling of a cottage garden, a mossy wall, or an old post … to imitate it minutely'.

Linnell painted this picture nearby, at what was then known as Kensington Gravel Pits. In it he advanced from localised studies to painting the gravel pits and the men who worked them with almost hallucinogenic sharpness and clarity, anticipating the searching truth to nature more usually associated with the later Pre-Raphaelites. It is also more uncompromising in its directness, simplicity and heroic treatment of labour than anything attempted by Constable, who sometimes introduced embellishments that he called 'eye salve' into his pictures as a concession to contemporary taste.

David Wilkie
(1785–1841)

The Village Holiday 1809–11
Oil on canvas
94 x 127.6
Purchased 1824

In his own field the Scottish-born Wilkie was the most innovative and influential painter of the nineteenth century. He reinvented for a modern audience the narrative subjects painted by Dutch artists two hundred years earlier and developed by Hogarth in the eighteenth century. The writer William Hazlitt called his pictures **'diaries, or minutes of what is passing constantly about us'**. Wilkie based them on close observation of real life, character and expression.

Always popular with rich collectors despite his sometimes 'low-life' subjects,

Wilkie sold this picture to John Julius Angerstein, whose collection was one of the first to be acquired for the National Gallery. Angerstein had philanthropic interests and the picture is a warning of the dangers of drink. Wilkie thought the English drank as hard as the Scots but enjoyed it less. Outside an inn on a public holiday a wife and child drag her reluctant husband home while his friends try to hold him back for a longer session. A man collapsed on the right predicts the inevitable consequences; Wilkie included his dog, which 'seemed to look ashamed of him'.

John Downman
(1750–1824)

Thomas Williams, a Black Sailor 1815
Chalk and pencil on paper
32.3 x 29.7
Purchased as part of the Oppé Collection
with assistance from the National Lottery
through the Heritage Lottery Fund 1996

Downman was a fashionable portraitist whose oils and smaller works in coloured chalks were in demand from 'the first people of rank and taste'. In fact, he became so busy that he started to make all his sitters look alike and was accused of depicting only two faces, one for women and the other for men. He responded to this criticism by focusing more on study from life, producing 'first studies' and separate drawings from models.

This remarkable portrait was drawn from life in Liverpool and carefully dated. Thomas Williams may have been a former slave who had taken the name of a British owner before being freed. Here he seems dressed as a gentleman, in jacket, shirt and cravat. Downman also included him in a watercolour, *Mr Wilberforce Abolishing the Slave Trade*, suggesting that he was known to William Wilberforce MP, who played a leading part in the Act of 1807 making slave-trading illegal in the British Empire. Downman's inscription on this drawing includes the comment that burnt umber 'perfectly expresses the complexion' of his sitter.

Samuel Palmer
(1805–1881)

Coming from Evening Church 1830
Mixed media on gesso on paper
30.2 x 20
Purchased 1922

Palmer embodied many of the characteristics of the Romantic movement – religious mysticism, historical nostalgia, love of pastoral nature, loathing of the modern world and a visionary imagination. He is among the best loved of British artists, especially for his earlier work made when he was a young man in retreat in the Kentish village of Shoreham with a group of friends, all admirers of Blake, who called themselves the 'Ancients'.

In fact, Palmer was far more conservative and conventional than Blake and subscribed to traditional, Tory ideas of an established rural order and the alliance of Church and State. The harsher realities of country life passed him by and his pastoral vision owed more to literary sources, from Theocritus and Virgil to Chaucer and Milton, than to things observed. In this little picture he evokes a timeless world of primitive innocence as the congregation leaves church after evensong. Their village paradise is tightly protected by hills and arching trees.

Richard Parkes Bonington
(1802–1828)

French Coast with Fishermen 1826
Oil on canvas
64.3 x 96.7
Purchased with assistance from the
Heritage Lottery Fund, The Art Fund and
Tate Members 2004

Bonington moved from Nottinghamshire to France as a young man, was trained in Paris by Baron Gros, revisited London with his friend Eugène Delacroix in 1825 and first exhibited there in 1826, when a critic, astonished by his work, asked 'Who is R.P. Bonington? We never saw his name before and yet here are pictures which would grace the foremost name in landscape art. Sunshine, perspective, vigour …'

This coast scene in Normandy was one of the London exhibits in 1826. Deceptively simply, it blends the genres of marine and landscape painting with a focus on working life represented by the fishermen, their wives, their children and their catch on the glistening beach in the foreground. Bonington's work had a transforming effect on his contemporaries on both sides of the Channel. His luminous landscapes, coast scenes, marines and historical compositions were soon admired by Turner, and his sparkling paint, which so marvellously conveys light and atmosphere, was compared by Delacroix to diamonds that delight the eye. He died tragically young.

John Everett Millais
(1829–1896)

**Christ in the House of His Parents
('The Carpenter's Shop')** 1849–50
Oil on canvas
86.4 x 139.7
Purchased with assistance from
The Art Fund and various subscribers 1921

Probably the most controversial painting produced by a member of the Pre-Raphaelite Brotherhood, this work invited the widespread criticism that the artist was playing fast and loose with sacred iconography. When exhibited at the Royal Academy in 1850, it was not given a title but was accompanied by an epigraph from the Old Testament prophet Zechariah: 'And one shall say unto him, What are those wounds in thine hands? Then he shall answer, Those with which I was wounded in the house of my friends.' Millais adopted this text to suggest an imaginary episode from the youth of Christ, and used the composition and its details to allude to the Crucifixion and the Anglican Church's two sacraments of Baptism and Communion.

In order to stress the symbolic significance of the subject, Millais emphasised the physical presence of every object in the painting. The sheep in the background were drawn from two heads obtained from a local butcher, and Millais squeezed drops of blood from his own hand and placed them on the palm of the young boy who posed as Christ in order to accentuate the tangibility of the wound. The figures were rendered with such realism that the public reaction was one of revulsion. Some critics felt it was sacrilegious to treat holy figures in such a loathsome way, especially types traditionally idealised such as Christ and the Virgin Mary. Charles Dickens, one of the picture's most vehement critics, described the Virgin as a wretch better suited to inhabit a cabaret or gin shop than a religious image.

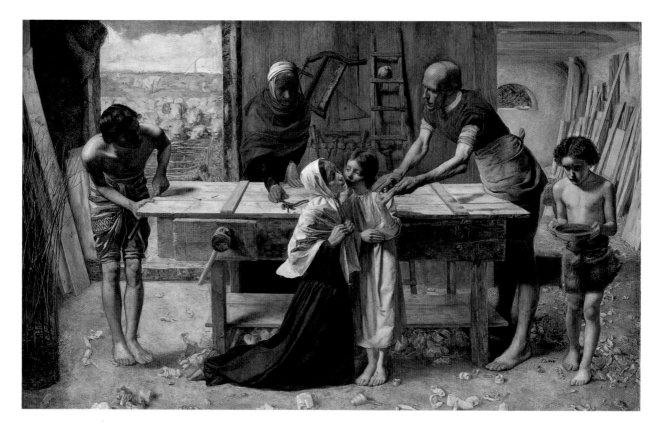

William Dyce
(1806–1864)

**Pegwell Bay, Kent – a Recollection
of October 5th 1858** ?1858–60
Oil on canvas
63.5 x 88.9
Purchased 1894

Dyce's 'Recollection' of the Kent coast at Pegwell, south of Ramsgate, operates on a number of levels. Stylistically it resembles the exacting attention to detail of the first phase of Pre-Raphaelitism. Though not himself a member of that group, Dyce here adopts the same kind of photographic precision to study the eroded shoreline and the worn cliffs, then renowned as a site rich in fossils. Mid-nineteenth-century interest in geology was encouraged by the writings of naturalists such as Sir Charles Lyell, Philip Henry Gosse, Charles Kingsley and G.H. Lewes. Dyce would undoubtedly have been aware of some of the new geological ideas arising from conclusions about why marine fossils were found above current sea level, which had begun to challenge conventional ideas of biblical time.

In the sky above this corner of England there is a slight blur denoting the passing of a comet. Newly identified earlier in 1858 by Giambattista Donati (1826–73), this phenomenon had been widely observed and also recorded by Samuel Palmer. Though this cosmic visitor served as a reminder of the insignificance of mankind, Dyce's painting also asserts the vitality of his own individuality, featuring several members of his family combing the beach in the foreground, as well as the figure of an artist, which is probably a self-portrait.

John Martin
(1789–1854)

The Plains of Heaven 1851–3
Oil on canvas
198.8 x 306.7
Bequeathed by Charlotte Frank in memory
of her husband Robert Frank 1974

History painting of the most high-minded and academic kind never really caught on in Britain, despite the best efforts of its promoters from Sir Joshua Reynolds to Benjamin Robert Haydon. But John Martin was hugely popular for his biblical spectaculars, which were toured throughout the country and reproduced in prints. Grand in scale and imagination, featuring fantastic landscape and architecture and crowded with minute figures, they were visually striking. They also struck a chord with millenarian notions of a coming apocalypse, then current in Nonconformist churches.

This is one of a triptych inspired by the description of the Last Judgement in the Book of Revelation, the final book of the New Testament. Dressed in white, the good, including a number of poets and artists, are assembling on the crest of a hill before being admitted into the celestial landscape beyond, a serene world of lakes, waterfalls and mountains.

Henry Wallis
(1830–1916)

Chatterton 1856
Oil on canvas
62.2 x 93.3
Bequeathed by Charles Gent Clement 1899

Thomas Chatterton (1752–70) famously wrote forgeries of medieval poems, but he was remembered for his melancholy life and suicide, which for artists of the nineteenth century represented the epitome of Romantic creative suffering. Wallis's picture shows the poet dying on his bed in a stereotypically derelict poet's garret, his manuscripts strewn by his side. The figure's posture, dishevelled clothing and beautiful features hint at an almost erotic atmosphere, and the viewer is certainly invited to look long and close at the picture. As Ruskin directed when the picture was exhibited, 'Examine it well, inch by inch.'

The Victorians made intimate, if often unconscious, connections between eroticism, death and poetic inspiration, and the cult that surrounded the teenage poet reveals much about their attitudes. The model used by Wallis for the figure of Chatterton was a friend, the struggling writer George Meredith, reinforcing the connection between the tragic poet and modern artists.

Dante Gabriel Rossetti
(1828–1882)

The Beloved ('The Bride') 1865–6
Oil on canvas
82.5 x 76.2
Purchased with assistance from
Sir Arthur Du Cros, Bt, and Sir Otto Beit,
KCMG, through The Art Fund 1916

Rossetti originally set out to represent Beatrice, the symbolic love of the medieval poet Dante's *Vita Nuova*, but later amalgamated this idea with the biblical Song of Songs and Psalm 45, words from both of which are inscribed on the frame of the picture: 'My beloved is mine and I am his. Let him kiss me with the kisses of his mouth: for thy love is better than wine' (Song of Songs); 'She shall be brought unto the King in raiment of needlework: the virgins her companions that follow her shall be brought unto thee' (Psalm 45).

The painting adopts the format of a religious icon in order to play provocatively on the senses in the appreciation of female beauty. Six figures are compressed into a shallow space as they process towards the groom who is positioned outside the frame waiting to receive the bride. She has Caucasian features, while the attendants are different ethnic types for which Rossetti used Romany, Indian and African models. The boy in the foreground may have been inspired by the figure of the black servant in Manet's painting *Olympia*, which Rossetti saw during a visit to the artist's Parisian studio in 1864. The arrangement of the figures suggests a racial hierarchy in which the bride is presented as supreme beauty in a 'Miss World' contest. However, the interfusion of different cultural elements, such as the kimono and Peruvian hair ornament adorning the bride, also communicate a synthetic idea of beauty. The flowers are similarly open to conflicting interpretations; the roses held by the foremost attendant allude to the rose-like complexion of the bride but also underscore the overall theme of intoxication.

John Frederick Lewis
(1805–1876)

The Siesta 1876
Oil on canvas
88.6 x 111.1
Purchased 1921

J.F. Lewis is an enigmatic figure in the history of British art. In 1837 he left England to travel through Italy, Greece and the Middle East, before setting up home in Cairo in 1841 where he remained until 1851. Very little is known about the time Lewis spent in Egypt, although the writer William Thackeray described the occasion when he met the artist living in great style in a large 'Mamluk' house in Cairo 'going about with a great beard and dressed up like an odious Turk'. On his return to England Lewis earned a reputation for images of Egyptian life painted in brilliant colour and detail in watercolour or oils. Many of these feature the harem, or women's private quarters, a place of particular fascination to Western viewers. While the harem signified all that was considered wrong with Near Eastern culture – its polygamy and sexual excess – it also represented a liberated eroticism that was seen to be lacking in Victorian society. Lewis's images of the harem parallel depictions of the 'separate sphere' of women in Victorian society, as if offering an equation between the gender prescriptions of East and West.

This painting dates from the very end of the artist's career and shows the extent to which he came to Westernise the idea of the harem. The image of a languid woman reclining in an interior with decorative props recalls the works of painters such as Frederic Leighton or J.W. Godward, who also used oriental accessories to enhance the sensuous mood of a scene. The *mashrabiya* screen in Lewis's painting recalls the one installed by Leighton above the Arab Hall in his London residence in the 1870s, and was probably painted from a 'prop' that Lewis brought back from the East.

James Abbott McNeill Whistler
(1834–1903)

Symphony in White, No.2:
The Little White Girl 1864
Oil on canvas
76.5 x 51.1
Bequeathed by Arthur Studd 1919

This picture shows the artist's mistress Joanna Hiffernan gazing into a mirror over a chimney piece at his house in Lindsey Row, Chelsea. The woman's white dress, prominently placed wedding ring and introspective expression hint at a narrative, but the liquid application of paint and bright notes of colour provided by the decorative oriental accessories establish competing areas of focus that deny clear interpretation. The girl's face is reflected in the mirror where it floats against a seascape. The reflected image seems sadder than the supposed real figure and the two faces fail to make eye contact. The mirror thus functions as a key device in blurring the boundary separating object from reflection and, by inference, material reality from illusion.

Before the painting left Whistler's studio for exhibition at the Royal Academy, the poet Swinburne composed a verse ballad, 'Before the Mirror', that parallels the mystery of the image:
Art thou the ghost, my sister,
White sister there,
Am I the ghost, who knows?
My hand, a fallen rose,
Lies snow-white on white snows, and takes no care.

Whistler had the poem printed on gold paper and pasted onto the frame in order to proclaim the unity of the arts in the creation of beauty. This aim was accentuated in 1867 when he gave the painting the additional title *Symphony in White, No.2*, reinforcing the idea that a visual image should communicate like music beyond the level of representation.

John Singer Sargent
(1856–1925)

W. Graham Robertson 1894
Oil on canvas
230.5 x 118.7
Presented by W. Graham Robertson 1940

Walford Graham Robertson (1866–1948) was a highly cultivated man: artist, illustrator, playwright, costume designer and collector. He owned an important collection of William Blake's works and presented and bequeathed many of them to the Tate, including the print on page 46.

Robertson met Sargent, a brilliant American portraitist, in 1894 and this picture was painted during the summer and early autumn of that year. It came about through Robertson's theatrical connections and his visits to the artist's Chelsea studio while accompanying his mother, whom Sargent was painting. Sargent was very taken by

Robertson's appearance on these occasions; he wore an elegant long overcoat and brought his old poodle Mouton with him. Before Sargent began work on this canvas he painted a smaller oil study in which he settled on Robertson's final pose. The long lines of Robertson's thin face, coat and carefully placed hands, one delicately holding a jade-topped cane, convey a real sense of all the relaxed elegance of a dandy of 1890s London. The dog with its pink ribbon joins in. In his reminiscences *Time Was* (London, 1931) the sitter noted that **'the dog and the overcoat seemed to be regarded [by Sargent] as my strong points'.**

Edward Coley Burne-Jones
(1833–1898)

The Golden Stairs 1880
Oil on canvas
269.2 x 116.8
Bequeathed by Lord Battersea 1924

Burne-Jones was a leader in the Aesthetic Movement and most of his subject matter came from classical or medieval sources. This picture is, at first sight, enigmatic; but the viewer soon becomes aware of the gentle mood of art and love that it evokes. Notably, it conveys soft sounds: bare feet walking on stone, maybe two or three whispered conversations, two girls lightly touching their stringed instruments. Wind and percussion instruments are silent. The Muses of classical mythology who presided over the arts and inspired their practitioners, including painters, poets or musicians, come to mind: some girls wear laurel crowns, an illusion to the laurel trees of the Muses' home on Mount Parnassus. The girls descend from a skyward point and on the nearby roof there is a pair of doves, traditionally a symbol of peace or love. A sprig of rosemary, symbol of fidelity, lies on the staircase. The staircase colour, gold, might even be seen as a reference to the first, or Golden, Age in the history of the world when man lived in harmony with all around him.

By the 1880s Burne-Jones's art was well known in Europe. When the young Pablo Picasso first left Barcelona in 1900, he intended to travel to London via Paris. He had seen reproductions of Burne-Jones's work and wanted to look at the originals but he got no further than Paris.

John William Waterhouse
(1849–1917)

The Lady of Shalott 1888
Oil on canvas
153 x 200
Presented by Sir Henry Tate 1894

Alfred Tennyson's poem 'The Lady of Shalott' (1832) tells of a cursed lady. Imprisoned in a tower on the 'silent isle' of Shalott, she is allowed to see the outside world only as a reflection in a mirror. She spends her time weaving, and some of the scenes that she has observed in the wall mirror are represented in the tapestry on her boat. One scene shows knights 'riding two and two'. It alludes to the fact that the lady 'hath no loyal knight and true'. But one day she sees a reflection of the 'bold Sir Lancelot' on his way to Camelot and turns to look at him: the mirror shatters, the tapestry falls off the loom and its weaver recognises her curse. Tennyson described it as a 'new-born love

for something, for some one in the wide world from which she has been so long secluded takes her out of the region of shadows into that of realities'.

The lady leaves her tower, and looks downstream to Camelot. She loosens the boat's chain and, lying down, sings her last song as the tide bears her away. One flickering candle symbolises her nearing death. Lancelot, at Camelot, is unmoved when he sees her dead. In his subtle reading of Tennyson's lines in his illustration of this final journey Waterhouse has produced a masterpiece. The fallen leaf on the lady's dress and the dying light speak eloquently of love unrequited.

Harry Bates
(1850–1899)

Pandora exhibited 1891
Marble, ivory, bronze and gilt
94 x 50.8 x 73.7
Presented by the Trustees of the Chantrey
Bequest 1891

The Greek myth of Pandora tells how Prometheus stole fire from Zeus, the king of the gods, to give it back to man. In revenge Zeus told Vulcan, the god of fire, to make a woman out of earth. Prometheus gave her life through fire. 'Pandora' means 'she with all gifts', having been given many by the gods. But Zeus wanted to bring misery to humankind, and in the box that Pandora carried were all the evils (as well as the gods' gifts) so far unknown to man. When she opened it, maybe out of curiosity, they escaped. By the time that Pandora shut the lid only Hope remained. In mythology Pandora was the first woman on earth and the destruction she let loose on man has

been compared with Eve's legacy after she ate the forbidden fruit. The moral of the first account of Pandora is that no one can escape the gods' purpose. Episodes in her creation are carved on the ivory box, made by Franz Nickolay, that Bates's Pandora holds. Bates leaves the box unopened, keeping the viewer in suspense.

Told through the medium of marble, the Pandora myth forged a powerful link between modern sculptors and the greatest art form of Ancient Greece. Hence Bates's advice to young sculptors quoted in the 1898 *Popular Handbook* to the Tate Gallery: 'master the secrets of those glorious conceptions – the figures from the Parthenon'.

Frederic, Lord Leighton
(1830–1896)

**And the Sea Gave up the
Dead Which Were in It** exhibited 1892
Oil on canvas
228.6 x 228.6
Presented by Sir Henry Tate 1894

The picture's title comes from verse 13 in chapter 20 of the New Testament Book of Revelation. The verse ends 'and death and hell delivered up the dead which were in them: and they were judged every man according to their works'. Leighton's subject is the final resurrection of man before the Last Judgement when all will stand before God. From the great (on the left a king rises out of his tomb) to the small (a child in his father's arms), everyone will be judged.

This work came out of an unused 1882–3 design that Leighton made for a mosaic in one of the spandrels of the dome of St Paul's Cathedral. The finished oil was commissioned by Henry Tate, to whom Leighton wrote in 1891. In the letter (now in the Tate archive) the artist looks back to the unfulfilled St Paul's commission and gives his reasons for returning to it: 'it was a grand and superb subject', unusual in contemporary art; his friends thought it the best design he had made; and it was 'the work which I should like to be remembered by in our National Gallery'. Leighton, President of the Royal Academy since 1878, here aspires to emulate Michelangelo just as an earlier president, Joshua Reynolds (see p.37), had said later generations of British artists should do.

Walter Richard Sickert
(1860–1942)

La Hollandaise c.1906
Oil on canvas
51.1 x 40.6
Purchased 1983

A man of sparkling wit and forceful personality, Sickert was probably the most important force behind early modern British painting. Pupil of Whistler, friend of Degas and acquaintance of Manet, he introduced Impressionism and Post-Impressionism to a younger generation of British painters – 'come to complete all your educations', as he once put it. Committed to Post-Impressionist realism, Sickert took for his subjects the ignored pathos of everyday life in street scenes, music hall audiences and stage acts. But it was in his charged, ambiguous pictures of figures in cramped interiors that Sickert touched real psychological depth.

In *La Hollandaise* he rejected traditionally ideal depictions of the nude; instead the naturalistic setting is a dusty London bedroom, the naked woman set in an inelegant posture on rumpled sheets. Sickert heightened this almost brutal intimacy by painting his model from a very close viewpoint, her face made anonymous by heavy shadows. The picture's distinctively rich, dark colouring and emotive surface are only barely finished, and paint has been used suggestively rather than to give fine detail. The uncompromising realism of the subject and its treatment were deeply shocking to an Edwardian audience, and in many quarters Sickert's art was reviled.

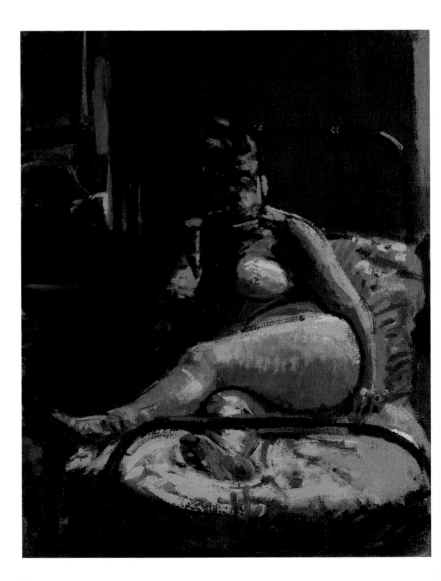

Duncan Grant
(1885–1978)

The Tub c.1913
Watercolour and wax on paper
laid on canvas
76.2 x 55.9
Presented by the Trustees
of the Chantrey Bequest 1965

Grant studied art in Paris in 1907 and knew both Matisse and Picasso, finding inspiration in their work. Like them, he was deeply fascinated by the energy and purity of form of African sculpture. This interest is echoed in *The Tub* in his nude's broad hips, tapering legs, flattened round breasts and the simple suggestion of her ribs, as well as the decorative hatched patterning of the background. Grant would also have known the writings on African art by Roger Fry, a fellow member of the Bloomsbury Group. Fry argued that what was commonly described as 'primitive' art possessed a raw, erotic passion that had been lost in traditional Western painting. Although he denied it, Grant's subject must have derived partly from the intimate bathing scenes of Degas, albeit treated in a wholly original and modern way. But the subject of the picture was almost certainly more directly inspired by watching Vanessa Bell washing. He had formed an intense and passionate relationship with her, and together they were at the forefront of early modern British art, introducing recent developments in France to a native audience. When first exhibited, their works frequently attracted either incomprehension or outrage.

Jacob Epstein
(1880–1959)

Torso in Metal from 'The Rock Drill' 1913–14
Bronze
70.5 x 58.4 x 44.5
Purchased 1960

Epstein grew up in New York and studied in Paris, before settling in London in 1905. Shortly before the First World War he was associated with the Vorticist group, at the forefront of modernism in Britain. The original plaster model for *The Rock Drill* was made in 1913, when the novelty of mechanisation was being explored by Vorticists, inspired by Futurism and Cubism on the Continent. It was exhibited at the London Group in March 1915. Epstein recalled: 'It was in the experimental pre-war days of 1913 that I was fired to do the rock-drill, and my ardour for machinery (short-lived) expended itself upon the purchase of an actual drill, second-hand, and upon

this I made and mounted a machine-like robot, visored, menacing, and carrying within itself its progeny, protectively ensconced. Here is the armed, sinister figure of today and tomorrow. No humanity, only the terrible Frankenstein's monster we have made ourselves into … Later I lost my interest in machinery and discarded the drill. I cast in metal only the upper part of the figure.'

In his creation Epstein sought to encapsulate the fearsome nature of the mechanised age and imagined *The Rock Drill* as a symbol of the new era, unchecked and hurtling towards the carnage of the First World War.

Wyndham Lewis
(1882–1957)

Workshop c.1914–15
Oil on canvas
76.5 x 61
Purchased 1974

Vorticism was a short-lived but radical movement that emerged in London immediately before the First World War. 'The vortex is the point of maximum energy', wrote the American poet Ezra Pound, who in June 1914 co-founded the Vorticist journal *Blast* with Wyndham Lewis. The journal opened with a manifesto that celebrated the machine age, and Britain as the first industrialised nation. '**Bless England, Industrial Island Machine, Pyramidal Workshop**', Lewis wrote. *Blast* makes it clear that *Workshop* is metaphorically – as well as literally – an image of industrial England. The painting epitomised Vorticism's aims, using sharp angles and shifting diagonals to suggest the geometry of modern buildings as if viewed from above. Its harsh colours and lines echo the discordant vitality of the modern city in an '**attack on traditional harmony**'.

The group's aggressive rhetoric, angular style and focus on the energy of modern life linked it to Italian Futurism, although it did not share the latter's emphasis on speed and dynamism. Artists associated with Vorticism included William Roberts, Edward Wadsworth, Jacob Epstein, Henri Gaudier-Brzeska, C.R.W. Nevinson and David Bomberg. The First World War demonstrated the devastating reality of pitting men against machines, and Lewis's attempts to revive the movement in 1919 came to nothing.

Stanley Spencer
(1891–1959)

Swan Upping 1915–19
Oil on canvas
148 x 116.2
Presented by the Friends of the Tate Gallery
1962

'Swan upping' takes place on the Thames every August. The Vintners and Dyers Companies own the river's swans by royal licence and take up the young birds each year for marking, by cutting their beaks twice.

The inspiration for the picture came while Spencer was in church in his native Cookham and heard people on the river. During the service 'the village seemed as much a part of the atmosphere prevalent in the church as the most holy part of the church … when I thought of people going on the river … it seemed … an extension of the church atmosphere'. Spencer later saw the swans being carried in carpenters'

bags and the girls carrying punt cushions to the river. He composed the scene from memory, its curious ambiguity emphasised by the men's hidden faces, their phallic, outstretched arms echoing the straining necks of the bound, powerful swans. Compositionally, the picture is a network of intersecting planes and lines. There are echoes of the Douanier Rousseau in the clear design of the sky and water, while the turbaned woman appears Florentine, as does the central figure on the bridge. While Spencer painted this scene, soldiers drilled outside his window. The First World War was getting closer, and he abandoned the half-completed picture to enlist.

Edward Burra
(1905–1976)

The Snack Bar 1930
Oil on canvas
76.2 x 55.9
Purchased 1980

Whether Burra's snack bar is in London, Paris or New York – all have been suggested as possible locations – it is the setting for a muted urban drama acted out under a harsh tungsten bulb. The light obscures a female figure outside in the street, and it seems likely she is a prostitute. The flashy outfit worn by the woman at the counter suggests that she is one too, and her solitary dining may be a way of plying for custom. This suggestion is strengthened by the lascivious sideward glance of the barman and the suggestive curling of the pink ham he is cutting. There is an underlying sexuality in the relationship of the two main figures, but the barman's attention, however, goes wholly unnoticed. The painting seems to speak of the perennial isolation of life in the city, which is exemplified by the mysterious, lonely male figure in the background. For all its apparently casual subject matter – a city bar, at night, in a cold season – *The Snack Bar* displays all the careful detail and composition that is typical of Burra. This is one of the very few oils that he made, his usual medium of choice being watercolour.

Ben Nicholson
(1894–1982)

1935 (White Relief) 1935
Painted wood
101.6 x 166.4
Purchased with assistance from the
Contemporary Art Society 1955

Because of their apparent austerity and relationship with modern architecture, Nicholson's 'white reliefs' have often been seen as cold and mechanistic. The art historian Kenneth Clark described them as 'spiritual beri-beri'. In fact, Nicholson emphasised the human side of the production of this work, which was carved out of a mahogany table top. The artist has left chisel marks still evident, which, with the uneven circle on the left, highlight the hand-made nature of the work. Nicholson envisaged a new way of living in which such traditional human values were central and there was a certain 'truth to materials'.

Writing about the work Nicholson pointed out: 'This relief contains one circle drawn by hand and one by compass and therefore represents the transition between the more freely drawn and more "mathematical" relief.' He noted how 'a square and a circle in art are nothing in themselves and are alive only in the instinctive and inspirational use an artist can make of them in expressing a poetic idea … You can create a most exciting tension between these forces.' According to the artist his move into relief came about as the result of a happy accident when a chip fell out at the intersection of two lines on one of his panels.

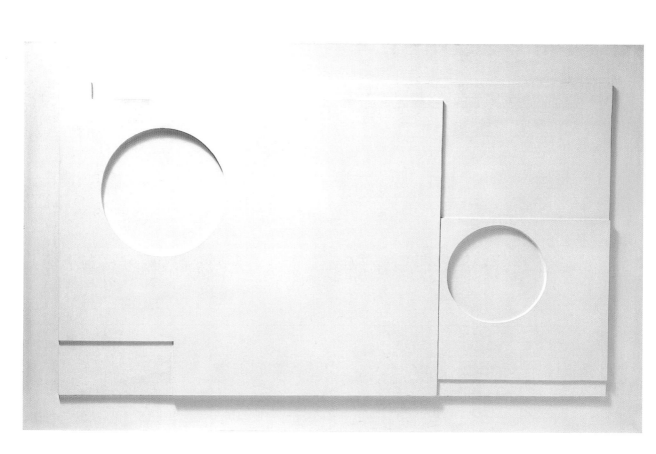

Eileen Agar
(1899–1991)

Angel of Anarchy 1936–40
Textiles over plaster and mixed media
52 x 31.7 x 33.6
Presented by the Friends of the Tate Gallery
1983

The blindfolded *Angel of Anarchy* was loosely based on an earlier head that Agar made in painted plaster, a portrait of her husband Joseph Bard. With this new work, Agar stated she wanted to create something 'totally different, more astonishing, powerful … more malign … [I]t has ostrich feathers for the hair, a Chinese silk blindfold, a piece of bark cloth round the neck and African beads at the back of the head, as well as occasional osprey feathers and a diamanté nose.' The African tapa cloth and the bead fringe were bought in antique shops, while most of the other materials were supplied from Agar's mother's wardrobe. *Angel of Anarchy* suggests the foreboding and uncertainty that Agar felt about the future in the late 1930s, and the gathering forces that would lead to war. She related that the title had a duel inspiration. The modernist critic Herbert Read 'was known to the Surrealists as a benign anarchist, so that is how I thought of the title "Angel of Anarchy", for anarchy was in the air in the late thirties'. But another impetus was coincidentally overhearing some workmen in the studio talking about the wood 'Archangel pine'.

Graham Sutherland
(1903–1980)

Green Tree Form: Interior of Woods 1940
Oil on canvas
78.7 x 107.9
Purchased 1940

One of his first major works, *Green Tree Form: Interior of Woods* was among several paintings of the period in which Sutherland invested natural 'found-objects' with anthropomorphic qualities. As such, with its fusion of landscape sources and abstract and surrealist vocabularies, it may be seen as epitomising a key aspect of the artist's work.

This was one of a number of variations of the same composition that derived from an uprooted tree lying across a grassy bank, close to the Milford Haven estuary in Pembrokeshire, south-west Wales. Sutherland discussed his use of such objects as fallen trees and roots in terms of 'paraphrase', and successive commentators have followed him in seeing metamorphosis as the principle behind the forms. He explained: 'The objects which I paint do, in fact, exist in nature. But ... my particular preoccupation in landscape is bound up with a desire to divorce some of the objects which one sees from their context ... I feel compelled to make the object 'once removed' from nature, thereby giving it a heightened form of realism ... I remove the traces of superficial reality or optical reality and try to retain the essence of the original object ... The prototype in nature has got to be seen through the terms of art. A metamorphosis has got to take place ... it is necessary to project or paraphrase the object.'

Paul Nash
(1889–1946)

Totes Meer (Dead Sea) 1940–1
Oil on canvas
101.6 x 152.4
Presented by the War Artists Advisory
Committee 1946

Paul Nash's use of landscape imagery as a vehicle for disturbing Surrealist fantasies had a considerable impact on artists of his generation. Nash supported the use of art as propaganda and during the Second World War was appointed as an official war artist, attached to the Air Ministry. He wanted his images of the defeated enemy 'to strike a blow on behalf of the RAF, apart from any triumph of art for its own sake'.

Totes Meer is based on a set of photographs taken by the artist of a dump for wrecked German aircraft at Cowley, near Oxford. The scene suggested a turbulent sea, an effect that Nash has heightened in his painted depiction, while also emphasising the composition's non-referential abstract qualities. The combination of bizarrely metallic wave forms and brooding colour establishes an unsettling tone and reveals a sense of tension between the natural world and industrial, modern life that was evident towards mid-century. As it had for other artists of his generation, the war provided Nash with the occasion to draw on the artistic innovations of the previous decades in work intended for a much broader public and produced with a real sense of social purpose.

Henry Moore
(1898–1986)

Recumbent Figure 1938
Green Hornton stone
88.9 x 132.7 x 73.7
Presented by the Contemporary Art Society
1939

This is one of the earliest works in which Moore depicted the female figure undulating like the landscape. It was commissioned by the modernist architect Serge Chermayeff to stand on the terrace of his home on the South Downs. Moore chose a reclining rather than an upright figure to harmonise with the horizontal lines of the long, low-lying, ultra-modern building. Moore explained: 'It was then that I became aware of the necessity of giving outdoor sculpture a far-seeing gaze. My figure looked out across a great sweep of the Downs, and her gaze gathered in the horizon. The sculpture had no specific relationship to the architecture. It had its own identity and did not need to be on Chermayeff's terrace, but it, so to speak, enjoyed being there, and I think it introduced a harmonizing element; it became a mediator between modern home and ageless land.'

Both visually and metaphorically, the figure acted as a bridge between the rolling hills and the new house. Like others, Moore used many native British stones at this time, absorbing ancient elements of the native landscape into modern form. Mined from a quarry near Banbury in Oxfordshire, the Green Hornton stone of *Recumbent Figure* seems itself to represent the ancient essence of the English landscape.

Francis Bacon
(1909–1992)

**Three Studies for Figures
at the Base of a Crucifixion** c.1944
Oil on board
Each 94 x 73.7
Presented by Eric Hall 1953

First exhibited in the spring of 1945 as the Second World War was drawing to an end in Europe, Bacon's triptych with its grossly distorted bodies provoked one critic to describe it as a reflection of **'the atrocious world into which we have survived'**. Since then it has become an icon of existential crisis representing the torture of the human condition. Bacon made an early reputation as an interior designer and painter in London in the period 1929–34 but then, unable to find a direction, painted only sporadically through the next ten years. Finally, in 1944 he completed *Three Studies for Figures at the Base of a Crucifixion*, with which, he said later, 'I began'.

The importance of the Crucifixion to Bacon was not particularly as a Christian image but as a focus for a particular view of humanity. In an interview with the critic David Sylvester, Bacon said: **'it was just an act of man's behaviour, a way of behaviour to another.'** In choosing the Crucifixion image and the triptych format as a vehicle for his vision of man, Bacon was drawing on one of the central and most important traditions in Western painting, that of the portrayal of human suffering. But it was intended as modern translation of a traditional subject; the strange beast in Bacon's vision seems both an embodiment and a perpetrator of suffering.

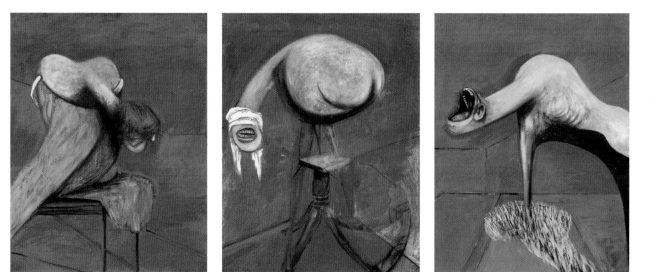

Barbara Hepworth
(1903–1975)

Group I (Concourse) February 4 1951 1951
Serravezza marble
24.8 x 50.5 x 29.5
Bequeathed by Miss E.M. Hodgkins 1977

With Henry Moore, Barbara Hepworth was the leading exponent of modern sculpture in Britain. Her work revived the tradition of direct stone carving, and marked a more vital approach to sculpture. This is the first of three similar pieces that can be seen as the culmination of Hepworth's figure studies of the late 1940s and early 1950s. They reflect the artist's dominant concern of those years: the formal arrangement of figures, and the symbolism of a more general harmonious human interaction. They may be thought to bring together the formalist values of her abstract sculpture and her social and political concerns of the 1940s. Hepworth associated *Group I* with her visit in June 1950 to the Venice Biennale, where she was exhibiting. She recalled: 'Every day I sat for a time in the Piazza San Marco … the most significant observation I made for my own work was that as soon as people, or groups of people, entered the Piazza they responded to the proportions of the architectural space. They walked differently, discovering their innate dignity. They grouped themselves in unconscious recognition of their importance in relation to each other as human beings.'

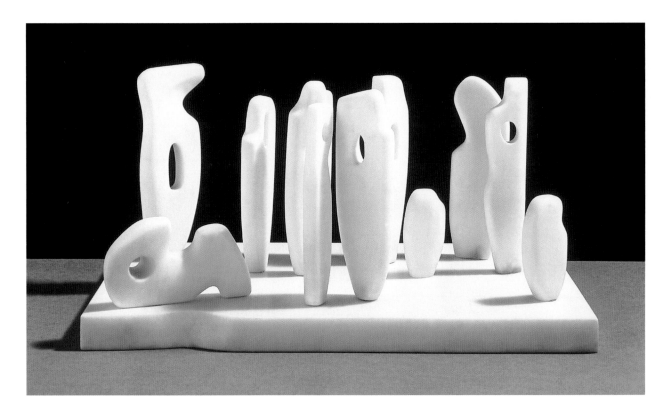

Victor Pasmore
(1908–1998)

Abstract in White, Green, Black, Blue, Red, Grey and Pink c.1963
Perspex and painted wood
81.5 x 91 x 46
Purchased 2005

Pasmore described his experience of seeing the 1946 Picasso exhibition at the V&A as an epiphany. The distortion and fragmentation of natural forms in Picasso's war paintings struck him as 'the final act in the alliance between humanism and natural philosophy'. What he meant by this was that in these pictures he saw natural objects distorted to an extreme degree as they were refracted through Picasso's imagination; they were, in short, a marriage of physical form and a human psychology. Intrigued by this realisation, Pasmore wondered how painting might develop henceforth. For him the solution did not lie in following Picasso, but in establishing a type of work in which 'the relation between artist and nature would be intrinsic and the imagery of painting a free and independent manifestation of this connection'. And so began his experiments with abstraction based on rules of proportion and harmony found in nature. He started making reliefs, whose structure was loosely built on formulae associated with natural growth patterns. This work is one of a handful of suspended constructions that Pasmore made around 1963. Appearing dazzlingly modern, it consists of sections of wood that project out of the front, back and one side of a clear plastic plane.

John Latham
(1921–2006)

Belief System 1959
Books, plaster, metal, light bulb and paint
on canvas
122.5 x 96.5 x 28
Purchased 2004

Belief System is one of a series of four similar works that Latham made in 1959 with the same title. They share a common structure with all Latham's paintings of the period, whose titles refer to the philosophical and scientific systems that he was seeking to undermine. Books have a special significance in Latham's work as a source of knowledge as well as of error. He referred to them as 'Skoob', the reversal of the word symbolising the subversion he aimed to effect on all they represented. His use of books in his assemblages of the late 1950s and early 1960s emphasises their dual nature: as physical objects held in a static state, books may be considered as witnesses of a momentary event taking place in the present, but at the same time they constitute repositories of knowledge that require an extension of linear time to be read. Like human bodies, they exist concurrently as unified wholes and as the containers of a mass of information, evoking spaces or concepts far beyond the immediate matter they are composed of.

In the *Belief System* works books embody processes of thinking contained within the immediate present. Latham believed the purpose of art was to recreate the lost relationship between the individual and the whole. To this end, he emphasised time-based process, or a language of events, over the static object.

Peter Lanyon
(1918–1964)

Thermal 1960
Oil on canvas
182.9 x 152.4
Purchased 1960

Peter Lanyon was the only native-born Cornishman among the leading figures of the St Ives School. His early work reflected the influence of modernist artists such as Naum Gabo, Ben Nicholson and Barbara Hepworth, who arrived in St Ives in 1939. The landscape of the Cornish coast provided a constant source of inspiration for his painting throughout his career. During the war Lanyon made abstract constructions but afterwards increasingly developed a landscape painting practice informed by American Abstract Expressionism. The artist had a one-man exhibition in New York in 1957 where he met and became friends with Mark Rothko.

Lanyon began gliding in 1959 and *Thermal* is one of a series of works that was partly inspired by his experience of flight. With its fluid swirls and strokes of paint, clear light and intense colour, this painting evokes not so much sea, sky and cloud as the artist's sensation of them. He later explained: 'The picture refers to cloud formation and to a spiral rising activity which is the way a glider rises in an up-current. There is also a reference to storm conditions and down-currents. These are all things that arise in connection with thermals.'

Anthony Caro
(b.1924)

Early One Morning 1962
Painted steel and aluminium
289.6 x 619.8 x 335.3
Presented by the Contemporary Art Society
1965

Between 1951 and 1953 Anthony Caro worked as Henry Moore's assistant but, influenced by new American art and art theory, he made a decisive break from Moore's example at the end of the 1950s. Where Moore was concerned above all with the idea of the image emerging from the sculptor's materials, whether it be clay, stone or wood, Caro developed an alternative approach centred around constructive methods using modern metals and a novel sense of lightness and space.

Early One Morning is a major example of the kind of sculpture that Caro had begun to develop by 1962. In this work Caro's arrangement of planes and lines along a horizontal axis gives greater freedom in creating different rhythms and configurations. His use of open forms, avoidance of any explicit figurative reference and insistence that the work be placed directly on the floor rather than on a pedestal stem from his desire that sculpture should be a 'direct' experience. The painting of the entire piece in one colour avoids the patination and monumentality found in more traditional kinds of sculpture and allows it to be read as a whole. The change in Caro's work marked a move away from the pessimism of the immediate post-war period and presented a response to the dominant American avant-garde.

Phillip King
(b.1934)

Tra-La-La 1963
Plastic
274.3 x 76.2 x 76.2
Presented by Alistair McAlpine
(later Lord McAlpine of West Green) 1970

Phillip King studied under Anthony Caro at St Martin's School of Art and, like his teacher, went on to work as an assistant to Henry Moore. His early works of the 1950s were generally small, made in clay or plaster, and of a robust Brutalist and Surrealist nature. King was led to revolutionise his sculptural practice in the early 1960s by a combination of exposure to new American painting and personal dissatisfaction with the figurative and expressionistic sculpture of the fifties. A visit he made to Greece around this time, which allowed him to study the relationship between ancient art and architecture, also fuelled his enthusiasm for abstraction.

King started to use sheet metal, fibreglass and colour to make abstract sculptures and embarked on a series of works exploring the form of the cone. *Tra-La-La* is the last work from a related series and comprises three separate stages of painted fibreglass, a movement echoed in the title. The abruptly truncated, twisting pink element evokes the illusion of the Indian rope trick and lends the work a light-hearted quality. This aspect, together with the use of fondant colours, subverted the monumental pretensions of other, more traditional, contemporaneous sculpture.

David Hockney
(b.1937)

A Bigger Splash 1967
Acrylic on canvas
242.5 x 243.9
Purchased 1981

David Hockney graduated from the Royal College of Art in the early 1960s and was initially regarded as a Pop artist. Drawing on the traditional genres of portraiture, landscape and still life, he has always featured colleagues, friends and lovers in personally significant places, including homes and holiday destinations, all of which lends his work the quality of memoir. A draughtsman, painter, printmaker, photographer, stage designer and outstanding portraitist, he visited California in 1963 and found there the inspiration for many of his works: a landscape and a way of life under perpetual sunshine.

David Hockney's *A Bigger Splash* is the last of three paintings made by Hockney in 1966–7 in which he sought to capture on canvas the sudden splash of water moments after a diver has broken the calm surface of a swimming pool. Hockney emphasised the way in which the splatter disrupts the stillness of the water by applying acrylic colours with rollers over the whole canvas and painting the central motif – the splash – with textured, staccato brush strokes. As he stated: 'I loved the idea, first of all, of painting like Leonardo, all his studies of water, swirling things. And I loved the idea of painting this thing that lasts for two seconds; it takes me two weeks to paint this event that lasts for two seconds.'

Richard Hamilton
(b.1922)

Swingeing London 67 (f) 1968–9
Acrylic, collage and aluminium on canvas
67.3 x 85.1
Purchased 1969

Richard Hamilton is a key figure in the development of Pop art in Britain. In the early 1950s he became a member of the Independent Group, a subsidiary of the Institute of Contemporary Arts in London, which was considered the seed of the Pop art movement in the UK. The group, which included artists and writers such as Eduardo Paolozzi and Lawrence Alloway, began to meet to discuss ideas around mass-produced urban culture, and concentrated on creating work and organising exhibitions strongly linked to themes of technology and the explosion of mass-media, or 'ad-mass', imagery.

Richard Hamilton's practice draws from and comments on a wide range of popular culture and current events. *Swingeing London* is the title of seven paintings and several prints based on a 1967 press photograph of Mick Jagger and Robert Fraser handcuffed together inside a police van, charged with the possession of drugs. The title comes from a comment by the judge: 'There are times when a swingeing sentence should be administered.' Hamilton combined it with a reference to a *Time* magazine article from April 1966 entitled *London: The Swinging City*, which mythologised the 'scene' in London.

Bridget Riley
(b.1931)

Fall 1963
Emulsion on hardboard
141 x 140.3
Purchased 1963

Bridget Riley studied at Goldsmiths College and later at the Royal College of Art, London, where her fellow students included Peter Blake and Frank Auerbach. Since the mid-1960s she has been celebrated for distinctive and vibrant abstract paintings that actively engage the viewer's perceptions and sensations. From 1961 to 1964 Riley worked with the contrast of black and white paint, with the occasional addition of tonal scales of grey. These early paintings reflect states of mind, dramatically shifting between composure and disturbance. Jackson Pollock's exhibition at the Whitechapel Gallery in 1958, which demonstrated the artist's concern for shallow and multi-focal pictorial space, had a profound effect on

Riley. The radical teaching methods of Victor Pasmore and Harry Thubron also proved instrumental in her development. From these artists Riley learnt to divorce form and colour from their descriptive roles, which enabled her to make the leap into abstraction.

Fall is one of the artist's key paintings from this early breakthrough stage. Here a single perpendicular curve is repeated to create a field of varying optical frequencies. In the upper part of the composition a gentle relaxed swing prevails, but the tension increases as the curve is rapidly compressed towards the bottom of the painting. The whole field verges on the edge of disintegration without the structure ever collapsing.

Gustav Metzger
(b.1926)

Liquid Crystal Environment
1965–6, remade 2005
Mixed media
Overall display dimensions variable;
duration 22 min
Purchased 2006

A pupil of David Bomberg (1890–1957) at the Borough Polytechnic, London, Gustav Metzger became a significant avant-garde figure in the late 1950s and early 1960s with his invention of the concept of 'auto-destructive art', a cultural response to the threat of destruction from nuclear war. Although it took a variety of forms, his auto-destructive art is best known through records of a number of performances in which Metzger painted acid onto nylon sheeting so that the 'support' would gradually disintegrate. His work influenced Pete Townsend of The Who – leading to the band's decision to destroy their instruments at the end of each performance.

Furthering his exploration of chemical processes in the production of art, Metzger began creating light projections using liquid crystals, first shown in 1966. The crystals were placed between glass plates and then heated. As they melted and then cooled, they took on a very intense coloration. Magnified in the projection, they created psychedelic effects, which were used as backdrops to performances by bands such as The Move and The Who. *Liquid Crystal Environment* was especially remade by the artist for Tate Liverpool's exhibition *Summer of Love: Art of the Psychedelic Era* (2005).

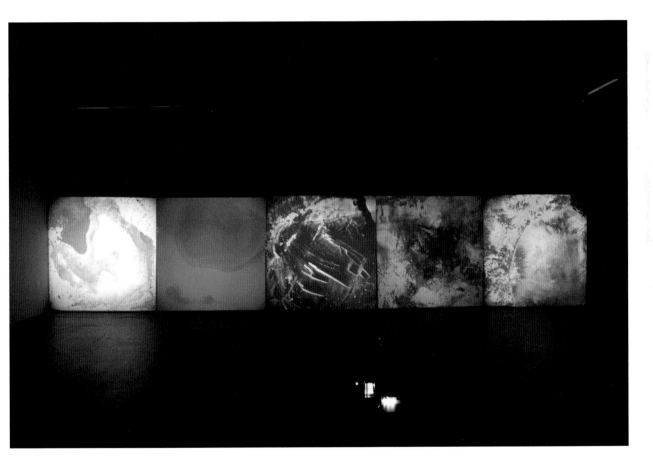

Barry Flanagan
(b.1941)

Four Casb 2 '67 1967
Canvas and sand
182.9 x 38.1 x 38.1
Purchased 1976

Since the mid-1960s Barry Flanagan has been making sculptures that challenge accepted conventions within sculptural practice. In explicit contrast to the generation of sculptors that preceded him, Flanagan began to work with soft materials, including sand and cloth, to investigate the ways in which these materials find their own form and can be influenced by simple manual activities such as pouring, stuffing, folding and stacking. He questioned the convention that sculptures should be rigid and permanently fixed by making works that could never be replicated exactly on different occasions.

Four Casb 2 '67 comprises four tapering, blue canvas sacks filled with sand. Although it is an independent work, it is usually displayed alongside two others, *Ringl 1 '67* and *Rope (Gr 2sp 60) 6 '67*. Whenever *Four Casb 2 '67* is exhibited, its canvas sacks are re-filled by pushing sand into each bag by hand, and so the work changes subtly each time it is made. This process also involves an exploration of the relationship between two substances, canvas and sand, which by their mutual support are transformed from shapeless materials into sculptures with solid form. By showing the three pieces together, Flanagan undermines their status as fixed, independent objects and focuses instead on their interrelationships.

Bruce McLean
(b.1944)

Pose Work for Plinths 3 1971
Photographs on board
75 x 68.2
Purchased 1981

McLean's work spans painting, photographs and performances as well as sculpture. As a student at St Martin's School of Art, London (1963–6), McLean was inspired by Anthony Caro, who had eliminated the sculptural requirement for a plinth, and began to think about ways in which traditional sculpture might be secondary to what it represented – the pose itself.

Pose Work for Plinths was originally conceived as a performance at the Situation Gallery in 1971, documentary photographs of which were published in the catalogue of McLean's one-day retrospective, King for a Day, held at the Tate Gallery on 11 March 1972. The artist also had himself photographed repeating the various poses in order to arrange the resulting prints into a grid. He made three versions of Pose Works for Plinths. All show the artist assuming poses on the same three plinths, comically attempting to achieve the postures held by the large reclining figure-sculptures of the great British sculptor, Henry Moore. McLean's work subverts both Moore and Caro. McLean further satirised the pose by forming the Nice Style 'pose art band' with Paul Richards in the early 1970s, taking on the posed personae of the members of rock bands as a subject for pastiche.

Patrick Caulfield
(1936–2005)

After Lunch 1975
Acrylic on canvas
248.9 x 213.4
Purchased 1976

Patrick Caulfield first came to prominence during the 1960s Pop art movement while studying at the Royal College of Art, London. Caulfield took his imagery from the world of the familiar and everyday but was also influenced by commercial and applied art, seventeenth-century Dutch still-life painting and Minoan frescoes. As a result of this eclectic, non-hierarchical approach to visual languages his paintings frequently incorporated a number of painterly approaches including photo-realism, colour field and *trompe-l'oeil*.

After Lunch was one of Caulfield's earliest works to combine different styles of representation, and the first to include a Photorealist passage. As in all Caulfield's paintings, the scene represented in *After Lunch* is imaginary. Here the high-focus realism of a photomural of the Château de Chillon contrasts strongly with the flat cartoon-like imagery that surrounds it. Caulfield deliberately made the relationship between the varying representational methods uneasy and ambiguous – an effect that is accentuated by the confusion between interior and exterior space. As with the pub and café interiors that Caulfield painted throughout his career, this scene demonstrates the artist's interest in spaces that are designed to make visitors feel at home but nevertheless retain an impersonal quality. The inclusion of the fondu pot, clichéd wooden interior and other 'Swiss' features in *After Lunch* takes the absurdity of such pretences to the extreme. Caulfield's characteristically kitsch and ersatz interior scenes are a metaphor for the deception and irony inherent in any form of representational art.

Howard Hodgkin
(b.1932)

Dinner at Smith Square 1975–9
Oil on board and wood
94.6 x 125.1
Purchased 1980

Howard Hodgkin's paintings exist in an indeterminate zone between representation and abstraction and often demonstrate an interest in the framing effects of the camera. Rather than attempting to express the outward appearance of objects or places, the artist strives instead to communicate a remembered memory from a specific experience. Colour and light are central to Hodgkin's process, and the artist has previously cited Corot, Canaletto and Turner as important influences. The 1970s saw major stylistic changes in Hodgkin's practice. In *R.B.K.* (1969–70), his portrait of R.B. Kitaj, Hodgkin used wood panel and painted over the frame for the first time. This device was to become his signature motif, one that he employed in order to reassert painting's object status. He soon eliminated figurative elements altogether, replacing them with stripes and dashes.

Dinner at Smith Square was based on the many evenings the artist spent dining with art-collector friends in Smith Square, London. Hodgkin has said that, for him, it conjures the scene of 'two old friends talking across their table below a small painting by Bonnard'. His paintings are often made over many years and incorporate the shifting viewpoints and perspectives of memory.

Hamish Fulton
(b.1946)

The Pilgrims' Way 1971
Photograph and text
150 x 225
Presented by Tate Members 2003

Hamish Fulton emerged in the 1960s as part of a generation of British artists seeking to expand the possibilities of sculptural practice. Variously described as a Conceptual artist, Land artist, Minimalist and photographer, Hamish Fulton prefers to characterise himself as a 'walking artist'. In over three decades Fulton has covered thousands of miles during several hundred walking journeys across numerous and diverse parts of the world.

Fulton regards *The Pilgrims' Way* as one of his most important early works. It is one of the first examples of the artist consciously making a defined walk a work of art, in this case along the ancient path between Canterbury and Winchester. The photograph originally featured in Fulton's first artist's book, *A Hollow Lane* (London, 1971), but was subsequently used by the artist as the lone signifier for the entire ten-day walk. Fulton does not remove or rearrange any objects found during his walks and this desire to leave the land unmarked by his presence differentiates him from other Land artists. In keeping with contemporary thinking on low-impact trekking, Fulton aims to leave no trace and explains that **'the single most important issue of our times is the condition of the planet'**.

THE PILGRIMS WAY

1971

A HOLLOW LANE ON THE NORTH DOWNS

ANCIENT PATHS FORMING A ROUTE BETWEEN WINCHESTER AND CANTERBURY

10 DAYS IN APRIL   A 165 MILE WALK

Richard Long
(b.1945)

Red Slate Circle 1988
Slate
37 x 400 x 400
Purchased with funds provided
by the Estate of Tom Bendhem 2004

Richard Long's art is centred on the relationship between man and nature. All his works stem from the basic activity of walking in the natural environment. During walks he may create temporary, *in situ* sculptures from natural materials to hand, assembling rocks or twigs in a circle or a line, which he later exhibits as photographs of the event. More permanent sculptures are created by bringing stones or sticks into the gallery space and laying them on the ground. Long's early interventions in nature in the late 1960s allied him with the movement known as Land art. With their simple, reductive and repetitive logic, his sculptures suggest a type of Minimalism that depends entirely on the human hand or body and on nature.

Red Slate Circle is a solid circle composed of rocks that have a flat underside, cut to sit evenly on the gallery floor. The remaining areas of the rock have been left unfinished resulting in a striking, jagged texture as the hunks of red slate point upwards into vertical space. Long brought the red slate from the border of Vermont and New York State in America. In installation the rocks are arranged carefully to fit within the predetermined diameter of the circle in such a way that no piece of slate touches another piece.

Tony Cragg
(b.1949)

Axehead 1982
Wood and mixed media
109.2 x 393.1 x 490.2
Purchased 1983

Tony Cragg, Richard Deacon, Anish Kapoor and Bill Woodrow form part of a prominent generation of British sculptors who emerged in the early 1980s. In contrast to the austere appearance of much Conceptual work of the previous decade, these artists offered a new diversity. They used a wide range of materials and imagery and began to invest them with personal narratives.

Richard Deacon refers to himself as a 'fabricator' and favours materials such as steel, wood or linoleum, with which he can draw attention to his role as builder. *For Those Who Have Ears #2* (1983) is one of a group of sculptures prompted by Deacon's desire to make works that refer to the

shape of an ear, and it relates to his interest in the way we channel our experience of the world through the senses. The creamy resin glue that has oozed out from between the layers of laminated wood creates a resolutely organic image, while also emphasising the work's 'fabricated' status.

Tony Cragg and Bill Woodrow are both drawn to the industrial landscape and often use materials found on the street or in junkyards. Cragg's *Axehead* (1982) consists of forty-nine separate objects arranged on the floor so as to form the fan-like outline of the head of an axe. It is typical of a group of works by Cragg that comprises multiple discrete components arranged in such a ❯

Richard Deacon
(b.1949)

For Those Who Have Ears #2 1983
Laminated wood and adhesive
273 x 400 x 110
Presented by the Patrons of New Art
through the Friends of the Tate Gallery 1985

way that they resemble another object. This approach has prompted a description of his work as a '**study of the relationship of the part to the whole**', an idea derived from particle physics.

In the early 1980s Woodrow began to give new meaning to familiar domestic appliances by peeling back their outer casing to form new objects. In *Twin-Tub with Guitar* (1981) he has cut a sculpture of an electric guitar from a discarded Hotpoint washing machine. This odd conjunction brings together two symbols of Western consumerism. Woodrow explains: 'The guitar was a pop icon and the washing machine was an everyday, domestic item.

So it was bringing the two things together like a slice of life.'

By contrast, Kapoor's sculptures deal with ideas of sexuality, spirituality and the sacred. *As If to Celebrate …* (1981) consists of three separate forms, each of which is coated with loose pigment. The forms suggest complex, organic structures that are both voluptuous and repelling. Kapoor has said: 'I don't wish to make sculpture about form – it doesn't really interest me. I wish to make sculpture about belief, or about passion, about experience, that is, outside of material concerns.'

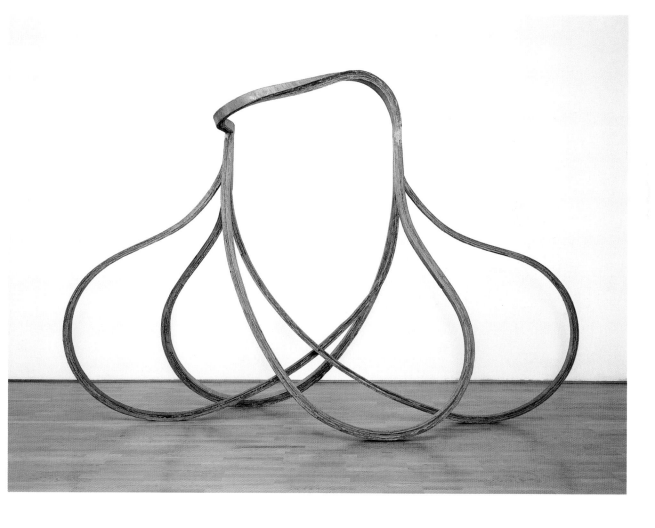

Anish Kapoor
(b.1954)

As if to Celebrate, I Discovered a
Mountain Blooming with Red Flowers 1981
Wood, cement, polystyrene and pigment
97 x 76.2 x 160; 33 x 71.1 x 81.3;
21 x 15.3 x 47
Purchased 1982

Bill Woodrow
(b.1948)

Twin-Tub with Guitar 1981
Washing machine
88.9 x 76.2 x 66
Purchased 1982

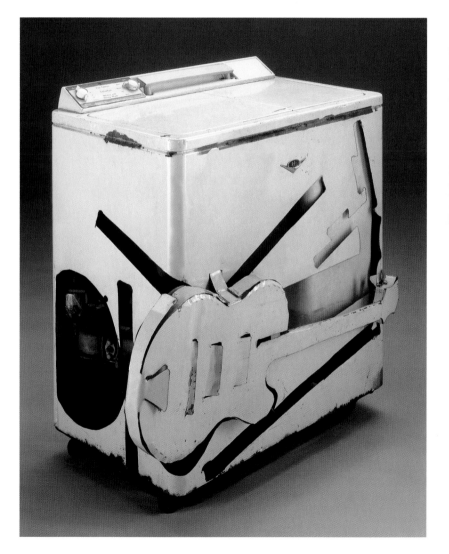

Cornelia Parker
(b.1956)

Thirty Pieces of Silver 1988–9
Silver and metal
Each 90 (approx. diameter)
Purchased with assistance from
Maggi and David Gordon 1998

Cornelia Parker is known for her often complex sculptures that change the nature of an object or material, sometimes through the use of extreme force. She extracts metaphorical associations from everyday objects, which are resurrected and transformed through her interventions. *Thirty Pieces of Silver* was the first large-scale work in which Parker subjected her materials to what she calls a 'cartoon death'. She has long been fascinated by the violence of cartoons, in which characters are repeatedly injured or killed only to reappear unharmed shortly after. *Thirty Pieces of Silver* consists of over a thousand flattened

silver objects that have been suspended in thirty circular forms about 30 cm from the floor. All the objects were ceremoniously crushed by a steamroller, recalling the artist's childhood practice of placing coins on the railway line to be flattened by passing trains. The title refers to the biblical story of Judas Iscariot's betrayal of Jesus in return for thirty pieces of silver. Parker has repeatedly used silver in her work because of its monetary and cultural associations. She has described how silver's ability to be both highly reflective when polished and dull and black when neglected gives it the potential to be both 'plus and minus in one material'.

Antony Gormley
(b.1950)

Testing a World View 1993
Cast iron
Each 112 x 48.5 x 107
Presented by the artist
(Building the Tate Collection) 2005

Testing a World View is a sculptural installation consisting of five identical iron figures bent at right angles at the waist. The figures are based on a cast made from the artist's body and are installed in varying positions related to the architecture of the space where they are on display. The figure's ninety-degree angle may be read as corresponding to the absolute laws of geometry. Gormley began using casts of his body for his sculptures in 1981 and continued to base his work on his own body during the 1980s and much of the 1990s. Early figures are encased in strips of roofing lead, joined with soldering lines that follow horizontal and vertical axes, constituting a type of grid. By contrast, the figures in *Testing a World View* were cast from iron. The lines on the bodies resulting from the casting process follow the contours of the body's limbs, conferring a more organic appearance. *Testing a World View* represents an attempt by the artist to challenge the single reading of a particular body posture, relating the body to architecture and other geometric formations. Like much of Gormley's work, it focuses on a single aspect of the body to express contradictory states of being.

Damien Hirst
(b.1965)

Pharmacy 1992
Mixed media
Dimensions variable
Purchased 1996

Religious imagery and pharmaceutical drugs have long been dominant features in Damien Hirst's work. For Hirst modern medicine, like religion, is one of a number of belief systems that are sustained by the fear of death.

The white Minimalist medicine cabinets and desks that comprise *Pharmacy* create a convincingly clinical atmosphere. This sterile quality is upset by the 'insect-o-cutor' hanging from the centre of the ceiling, the prospect of dead flies, and the four bowls of honey that are situated on kick stools below and lure the creatures to their brutal death. In a similar manner to the honey, the

pharmaceutical drugs, with their inevitable side effects, could be seen to represent a seductive and impermanent means for escape from sickness and pain. On the counter four liquid-filled glass apothecary bottles represent the elements of earth, air, fire and water. Their inclusion serves as a reminder of ancient, and perhaps misguided, practices of treating and healing the body. For his part, Hirst maintains a belief in the transformative powers and honesty of art. In *Pharmacy* the artist alludes to a hypocritical situation where blind faith and confidence in medicine might also run parallel to a disbelief and mistrust in art.

Douglas Gordon
(b.1966)

10ms-1 1994
Video
229.5 x 306 (unconfirmed);
duration 20 min 57 sec
Purchased 1997

Douglas Gordon's work investigates the mechanics of perception, both psychological and visual. Many of his film-based works break the medium down through slow motion and projection onto large free-standing screens (sometimes more than one at a time) in order to draw the viewer's attention to hitherto unseen details. These techniques challenge the construction of meaning through memory as well as the viewer's relationship, both physical and psychological, with the moving image. In the early to mid-1990s Gordon produced a series of works involving projections of pre-existing film footage, which he manipulated and projected onto large free-standing screens. In the most famous of these he slowed down Alfred Hitchcock's film *Psycho* to a duration of twenty-four hours, calling the piece *24 Hour Psycho* (1993). He made several works using material from medical films recording psychological malfunction. *Hysterical* (1994–5) is a fragment of a medical demonstration film of 1908 enacting techniques for the treatment of female hysteria.

The footage of *10ms-1* is a fragment of a medical film from the First World War documenting the attempts of a psychologically injured man to stand up and walk. These symptoms of war trauma are the physical manifestations of what later came to be understood as male hysteria. *10ms-1* is a video projection on a large free-standing screen.

Tracey Emin
(b.1963)

**Outside Myself (Monument Valley,
reading 'Exploration of the Soul')** 1995
Photograph on vinyl
122 x 183
Presented by Tate Members 2004

Inspired by the German Expressionists, who often portrayed their feelings and intimate relationships, Emin's work conflates her life with her art. Her practice includes performance and photographic records of performances. *Outside Myself* results from a trip Emin made to the United States in 1994 when she drove from San Francisco to New York, stopping off along the way to give readings from her book, *Exploration of the Soul* (1994). The photograph shows the artist sitting in an upholstered chair in Monument Valley, a location in the Arizona Desert, holding her book. Emin gave her readings sitting in the chair, which she had inherited from her grandmother. Onto it she appliquéd words and sections of text

referring to her family relationships. As she crossed the United States, Emin stitched the names of the places she visited onto the front of the chair. She subsequently presented the chair as an artwork in its own right entitled *There's a Lot of Money in Chairs*, 1994.

Emin has used large-scale photographs of herself to record and express moments of emotional significance in her life, frequently making reference to her career as an artist. *Outside Myself* brings together the multiple parts that make up the Emin artwork – the artist's inner life as inspiration and subject of the work, the artist as performer, and the work itself as a relic of the processes of creation and consumption.

Sarah Lucas
(b.1962)

Pauline Bunny 1997
Mixed media
95 x 64 x 90
Presented by the Patrons of New Art
(Special Purchase Fund) through the
Tate Gallery Foundation 1998

Sarah Lucas specialises in challenging gender stereotypes through a play on conventions of representation and framing, specifically through the language and media of popular culture. She frequently appropriates everyday objects, particularly domestic furniture and food to make sculptures about sexuality and death.

Pauline Bunny was originally a component of a larger installation entitled *Bunny Gets Snookered* in which eight similar mannequins were arranged on and around a snooker table. Each 'bunny' wears differently coloured stockings corresponding to the colours in a set of snooker balls. *Pauline Bunny*, in its black stockings, corresponds to the highest value snooker ball. The black stockings are traditionally the most sexually alluring of the selection of colours, connecting this representation of a woman to the image of a seductress. This is reversed by the passivity of the floppy, stuffed body and the office chair to which it is clipped, providing an emblem of secretarial submissiveness. The title of the installation reinforces the reading of disempowerment: to be 'snookered', in the language of the game, means to be prevented from hitting your own balls and therefore from scoring. The bunny's unhelpful slump, her sagging form and literally empty head provide a comic antithesis to her traditional namesake (the *Playboy* bunny) and subvert stereotypical masculine desire. If femininity has been objectified, here that process of objectification is itself revealed to be ridiculous.

Mona Hatoum
(b.1952)

Incommunicado 1993
Metal cot and wire
126.4 x 57.5 x 93.5
Purchased with funds provided
by the Gytha Trust 1995

Mona Hatoum's work is based on a tension between attraction and fear. Influenced by her experiences of political conflict in the Middle East, in the early and mid-1980s she made video and performance pieces that focused on her body and identity. In 1989 she began to abstract her political themes, creating sculptural installations. In these, metal structures based on domestic furniture suggest fences, cages, compartments and racks, evoking themes of dispossession, displacement, claustrophobia and controlled violence. She frequently uses the formal device of the metal grid, with its 1960s Minimalist associations, as a metaphor for the ordering and control of states of extreme emotional violence and distress, rendering their expression more acute.

Incommunicado is a sculpture based on an altered infant's cot. The springs have been replaced by tautly stretched, fine cheese wires. Free from padding or mattress, the cold, hard, metal form of the cot has been honed down to its most bare and chilling structure. The potentially lethal wires anticipate acute pain, the result of the sadistic violence of a parental torturer. The title describes a place where communication and therefore love are no longer possible. *Incommunicado* provides a metaphor for the plight of many political prisoners who are incarcerated and tortured in places where their voices cannot be heard.

Susan Hiller
(b.1940)

From the Freud Museum 1991–6
Mixed media
Dimensions variable
Purchased 1998

American-born artist Susan Hiller has lived and worked in Britain for over twenty years. Her work across all media often takes as a starting point what she terms 'cultural artefacts'. Hiller consistently focuses on ideas, events or objects that have been ignored or forgotten.

In *From the Freud Museum* Hiller has applied the procedures of museum classification and presentation to a diverse range of boxed objects. Inspired by Sigmund Freud's collection of antiquities and artefacts, she installed a series of objects – items as diverse as water from a sacred spring in Ireland and stones collected from Mount

Sinai – into small buff cardboard boxes in glass display cases. Each object is accompanied by a visual or literary representation and the installation is completed with the projection of the video *Bright Shadow*, which itself presents a hard-to-decipher image. Hiller invites the viewer to rediscover these seemingly trivial miniatures, to reconsider their significance in both cultural and personal terms. Thus she turns those objects into tools to reveal hidden content. The relationship between the public and formal presentation of objects and the personal and emotional response to them is typical of Hiller's installations.

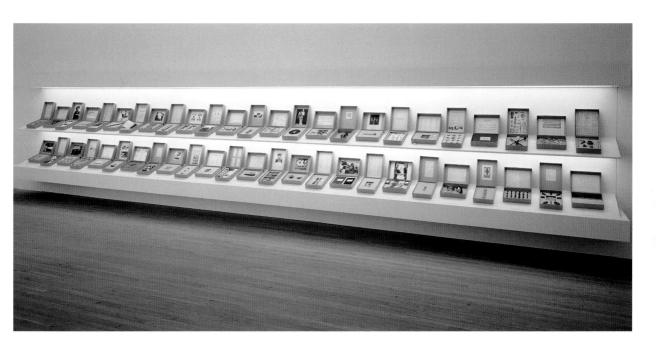

Angela Bulloch
(b.1966)

West Ham – Sculpture for Football Songs
1998
Mixed media
Dimensions variable
Purchased 2006

Since the early 1990s Bulloch has been creating clinical and cool-looking installations reminiscent of Minimal art. These include elements such as translucent cubes or spheres whose coloured lights are activated by the viewer or modified by the passing of time: they go on and off or change colour in reaction to a predetermined mechanical sequence or the behaviour of the people around them.

West Ham – Sculpture for Football Songs, an early light work by Bulloch, is an installation of four wall-mounted Belisha beacons and is one of a number of works that incorporate this recognisable item of British street furniture. The colours of the light bulbs are light blue and burgundy, like the West Ham football team strip. *West Ham – Sculpture for Football Songs* reacts to the sound levels of the gallery where it is installed: its sequence of flashing lights is triggered by acoustic signals received by a microphone that activates a light-switching mechanism. Hence, the louder the environment, the faster the light sequence. Initiating a dialogue between the work and the space it occupies, Bulloch creates a language of cause and effect, and raises awareness of the influence in behaviour exerted between people and objects.

Martin Creed
(b.1968)

**Work No.232: the Whole World
+ the Work = the Whole World** 2000
Neon tubing
50 x 1550
Presented by the Patrons of New Art
(Special Purchase Fund) 2001

Martin Creed's practice is concerned with the tension between something and nothing, with what exactly constitutes an artwork, and the value of that work in relation to the world around it. Like many British artists who emerged in the 1990s, Creed echoes the strategies initiated in the 1960s by Conceptual artists such as Lawrence Weiner (b.1942) and Joseph Kosuth (b.1945), who sought to highlight the ambivalent position of art within society.

Equations, conundrums and aphorisms are typical of Martin Creed's investigation into the ways in which objects and ideas fit together. *Work No.232* was commissioned as part of a programme of exhibitions in 2000 to mark the transformation of the Tate Gallery's Millbank site into Tate Britain. The meaning of this neon sculpture is caught in a tautological loop that continually frustrates all attempts to arrive at a final and fixed meaning. Creed first used the equation for *Work No.143* in 1996, where he wrote it in ink on a sheet of paper. The word 'work' may refer to an artwork as well as the ordinary world of work, but in either case its relative value ultimately remains ambiguous.

Rachel Whiteread
(b.1963)

Untitled (Stairs) 2001
Mixed media
375 x 22 x 580
Purchased from funds provided
by The Art Fund and Tate Members 2003

Rachel Whiteread's practice is based on casting the internal or negative spaces of domestic furniture and architectural structures. Her casting processes transform emptiness into solid objects, emphasising the geometry of structures that human bodies interact with daily. Casts made in rubber may be opaque or clear with a range of evocations that include dead matter, flayed skin and urine; those made in clear resin have more watery and sublime associations, while plaster produces simple white blocks emphasising pure form.

Untitled (Stairs) is one of three casts of staircases that Whiteread made in a building in Bethnal Green, London E2, which she purchased as a home and studio in 1999. Originally a synagogue, the building had been reconstructed in the 1950s after bomb damage in the Second World War and became a warehouse in the 1970s. In addition to the staircases, she cast the synagogue floor and the interior spaces of two purpose-built apartments on the first floor. In making this work, Whiteread cast the surface of the stairs, including three square-shaped landings as the stairs zigzag down the stairwell, and the space above them. The solidified space has been rotated by 90 degrees so that it stands on an edge that would have been a wall in the house, providing a visual conundrum.

Chris Ofili
(b.1968)

The Upper Room 1999–2002
Oil paint, acrylic paint, pencil, ink,
polyester resin, gold leaf, glitter, map pins
and elephant dung on linen, with elephant
dung supports
Each of 12 canvases 183.2 x 122.8;
larger canvas 244.2 x 183
Purchased with assistance from
Tate Members, The Art Fund and private
benefactors 2005

Chris Ofili's *Upper Room* consists of thirteen paintings displayed in a specially constructed space designed in collaboration with the architect David Adjaye. The dark, walnut-panelled room, approached through a dimly lit corridor, provides a chapel-like setting for the individually spotlit paintings. The arrangement of twelve canvases flanking a thirteenth larger one suggests Christ and his Apostles. The paintings radiate in the space: a luxuriant combination of shapes and textures built up from paint, resin, glitter and gold leaf. Elephant dung – a signature element in Ofili's work – is also incorporated as a material and is used as a support to prop each canvas against the wall.

All thirteen paintings show a rhesus macaque monkey, and each is dominated by a different colour, identified in Spanish on the elephant dung supports. In a text that accompanied the work's first exhibition, a conservation biologist described the rhesus macaque as 'loud, active, entertaining, fearsomely intelligent – the consummate cheeky monkey'. She also pointed out how rhesus monkeys have been venerated in certain religions, and observed that 'monkeys may be godless but ... rhesus macaques display a deeper degree of compassion for each other than do human beings'. With this work Ofili raises questions about the relationships between civilisation and untamed nature, between the religious and the secular.

Jim Lambie
(b.1964)

Zobop 2003
Multicoloured vinyl tape
Dimensions variable
Presented by Tate Members 2006

Jim Lambie's assemblages are made from the cultural detritus of everyday life. With its reference points in music and 1970s and 1980s youth culture, Lambie's often psychedelic treatment of discarded objects imbues his sculptural work with an energy and emotion that augments rather than masks the object's inherent qualities. While his pieces are often formally rigorous, Lambie is more concerned with the viewer's immediate encounter with the work, prioritising sensory engagement over intellectual response.

Such is the case with *Zobop*, part of Lambie's ongoing series of floor-based interventions. Created with narrow strips of brightly coloured adhesive vinyl tape, each installation of the work is site-specific, with the pattern informed by the architectural features of the space in which it is installed. Starting at the edges of the room, Lambie works his coloured stripes inwards until they collide in the centre of the floor, amplifying the importance of columns, doorways and alcoves and transforming the mood and character of the interior. In the simple act of dissolving the room's apparent boundaries, Lambie provokes the viewer to consider a psychological space beyond the physical environment.

Gilbert & George
(b.1943, b.1942)

Fates 2005
Laser print on paper
426 x 760
Purchased with assistance from
Tate Members 2006

Gilbert & George have maintained a provocative and transgressive presence in art for almost forty years. Since the 1980s they have produced large-scale photo works that deal with fundamental themes mediated through complex, ambiguous and personal references. These themes range from multicultural urban Britain to various national stereotypes and taboos, and the artists' sexuality and bodily functions.

Fates is one of the twenty-five works comprising the *Gingko Pictures* series, of which this is the centrepiece. This is the first series in which the artists have exclusively used digital editing techniques, which in itself is an allusion to seriality and mass production in contemporary society. The effect is a rich patchwork, where the intensely coloured and perfectly printed panels resemble profane stained-glass windows. The elements in this work make reference to the multiracial character of Britain but also to the fear of difference. Many of the motifs are recognisably associated with Eastern religions, but the references are non-specific and mutated, resembling 'the East' as seen through the architectural and cultural fantasies of Las Vegas. These generic references are given specificity in relation to the cultural context of Brick Lane and the East End, which has been the basis of the artists' work since they moved there in the late 1960s.

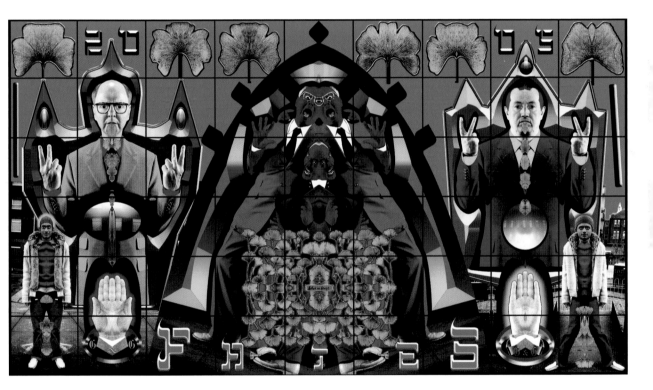

Tacita Dean
(b.1965)

Palast 2004
16mm film, audio
Duration 10 min 30 sec
Presented by Tate Members 2006

Mark Wallinger
(b.1959)

Sleeper 2004–5
Mini DV transferred to DVD
Duration 2 hr 30 min
Presented by Tate Members 2006

Over the past decade, a growing number of British artists have been using film and video, exclusively or alongside their work in other media. The range of approaches adopted includes the reconfiguration of existing films or archival footage, documentary-style recordings of action or performance, and projected images using a static frame. The greatly expanded possibilities offered by the medium allow contemporary artists to address concerns such as globalisation, modernisation, politics and identity in subtle and poetic ways.

Several of these concepts are explored in Tacita Dean's *Palast*, which documents a reflected image on the vast banks of orange-glass windows that clad Berlin's Palast der Republik. Erected on the site of a baroque royal palace, which was bombed and finally demolished in 1950, this defiantly modernist structure, built to house the East German parliament, was itself scheduled for demolition at the time of filming. Dean's recording of the reflections of sky and neighbouring buildings on the windowed facade of the Palast is characteristically understated and yet eloquently evokes the artist's continued concern with memories, outmoded ideologies and the erasure of history.

Mark Wallinger's *Sleeper* takes place in another iconic Berlin building, the Mies van der Rohe-designed Neue Nationalgalerie. Dressed in a faux-fur bear suit, Wallinger occupied the empty upper galleries of the building for several hours over nine consecutive nights. In unedited footage filmed on three cameras on a single night, the artist is seen pacing the glass-walled galleries, returning onlooker's stares and ❯

Steve McQueen
(b.1969)

Caribs' Leap/Western Deep 2002
Three-screen video projection, audio
Durations 28 min 53 sec, 24 min 12 sec,
12 min 6 sec
Purchased 2005

Rosalind Nashashibi
(b.1973)

Hreash House 2004
Digibeta master
Duration 20 min
Presented by Tate Members 2006

sometimes disappearing from view. In much of his work Wallinger interrogates contemporary society's traditions and values, ranging from Britain's class system to institutionalised religion. His portrayal of the bear, Berlin's heraldic symbol, as a tragicomic figure, aimlessly wandering in the modernist space, is a subtle allusion to nature, culture and politics, as well as the generally alienating nature of contemporary society.

Steve McQueen's video works often form a post-colonialist critique, as in *Caribs' Leap/Western Deep*, two works shown together as a three-screen installation. Filmed on the Caribbean island of Grenada where McQueen's parents were born, *Caribs' Leap* memorialises a historical incident in 1651 when the last independent Carib Indians leapt to their death to avoid

colonisation by the French. *Western Deep* follows the descent of predominantly black miners into the claustrophobic confines of the world's deepest gold mines in South Africa. The juxtaposition of the films forms an affecting lyrical allegory of descent, endurance, desperation and redemption.

Rosalind Nashashibi also addresses social and political structures within her work. In *Hreash House* she documents the daily activities of an extended family living in Nazareth. By simply following the occupants of a house as they prepare food, eat, clean and sleep, Nashashibi avoids any overt or didactic commentary. Instead, she focuses on details such as intricate textile patterns and particular arrangements of objects, allowing these to convey a sense of humanity and order within the apartment, which contrasts with the political chaos of the locality.

Richard Wentworth
(b.1947)

Making Do and Getting By
1974–2005 and
Occasional Geometries
1973–2005
100 colour prints on paper mounted
on glass, on aluminium shelf
242 x 345
Purchased 2005

Richard Wentworth is best known for his sculptures, which typically transform or subvert the role of mundane objects, maintaining their form while lending them a new or double identity. In two series of photographs he has been making since the mid-1970s under the titles of *Making Do and Getting By* and *Occasional Geometries*, he captures similar configurations in everyday life. The first series, documenting various objects left out on the street, forms a survey of improvisational repairs and provisional props – a discarded glove propped like a finial on a fence or a kitchen chair reserving a parking space. In *Occasional Geometries* Wentworth focuses on accidental formal patterns, such as those created by misaligned tiles or stacked sheets of corrugated iron.

The work in Tate's Collection consists of a selection of one hundred images taken from both series and shares with Wentworth's sculptural work a concern with improvisation and surprising and unexpected transformations. Despite their public nature, the arrangements Wentworth's camera captures are, for the most part, created without thought of an audience. Rather, being variously incidental or unintentional, or made out of some personal necessity or desire, they celebrate the personal, provisional, fortuitous and casual encounter, combining the touching pathos and liberating good humour that informs Wentworth's own constructions.

Jeremy Deller
(b.1966)

**The Battle of Orgreave Archive
(An Injury to One is an Injury to All)** 2004
Mixed media
Overall display dimensions variable
Presented by Tate Members 2005

Working in many capacities – as an artist, curator, producer and publisher – Jeremy Deller conceives and generates works and projects that draw out connections between the activities and ideologies of seemingly disparate groups. Deller's practice, which is often collaborative or participatory, is also characterised by its political engagement. Ranging from staged events to posters and collections of objects, his work provides unique historical and psychological insights into contemporary culture.

In one of his most high-profile works, *The Battle of Orgreave*, Deller created a re-enactment of the controversial clash that occurred between coal-miners and police in South Yorkshire on 18 June 1984 at the Orgreave coking plant near Sheffield. At the

height of an industrial dispute that lasted almost a year the violent confrontation between some five thousand miners and eight thousand police had culminated in a cavalry charge by mounted police through a nearby village. In a project produced by Artangel, Deller restaged the clash using a cast of military re-enactment enthusiasts along with people from the local community, many of whom had participated in the original incident. The archival materials from the project, including a documentary film of the event, ephemera, wall drawings, photographs and interviews, provide an alternative account of this formative moment in recent history in comparison to the distorted reports that appeared in the contemporary media.

Tomma Abts
(b.1967)

Noeme 2004
Acrylic and oil on canvas
48 x 38
Purchased 2006

In her enigmatic paintings Tomma Abts explores the possibilities of an abstract language of form and makes the narrative of the painting process her subject. Abts forgoes source material or preparatory drawings and begins with no preconceived idea of the final result. Instead, working consistently to a format of 48 x 38 cm in acrylic and oil paint, she allows her paintings to take shape through a slow method of layering and accrual. That the resulting works appear calculated belies a practice informed by intuition and contingency. The artist describes the finished works as 'a concentrate of the many paintings underneath' and 'images of thought', each functioning as an autonomous object revealing the visible traces of its construction. Despite existing in

two dimensions, Abts's paintings possess a physicality that is enhanced by their optical three-dimensional quality. Paint is thickly applied in places, sometimes creating ridge-like reliefs and giving her forms sculptural definition that at times is emphasised by areas of *trompe-l'oeil* shadow beneath.

Abts's paintings often begin to take on figurative qualities. In *Noeme* the interlocking linear elements are suggestive of planets or their halos. The ambiguous nature of Abts's forms undermines and makes redundant traditional distinctions between abstract and representational painting. Her desire for her works to exist on their own terms, without supplementary reference, is reinforced by their titles, which are randomly selected from a German dictionary of regional first names.

Ceal Floyer
(b.1968)

Double Act 2006
Mixed media
Dimensions variable
Purchased 2006

Ceal Floyer's installations are often inconspicuous or unassuming – a light switch that on closer inspection turns out to be a projected image, for example, or a 'monochrome' fashioned from a shopping receipt listing only white-coloured items. In these apparently simple gestures she makes sophisticated use of strategies from such art-historical precedents as *trompe-l'oeil* painting, Marcel Duchamp's ready-mades, and Conceptual and Minimalist art of the 1960s, often wittily commenting on art itself in the process.

Several of these strategies underpin *Double Act*. At first appearance, a set of heavy red velvet stage curtains, highlighted by two spotlights, seems to herald the opening act of a performance. The evidence of a single stage light in the gallery reveals the doubling of the spotlight to be an optical effect, as the point where the curtains and floor meet forces the beam onto two separate focal points. But the curtains themselves are also an illusion, the result of a photographic transparency projected from the spotlight itself. The closed curtains, which seem to promise an act, turn out to be the act itself. As in so much of her work, Floyer consistently thwarts our assumptions about what it is we are seeing and, in doing so, questions the very nature of both representation and reality.

Index

Copyright

Photography credits

Unless otherwise stated, photographic copyright is held by Tate

p.19 Tate Photography / Mark Heathcote and Sam Drake

pp. 84, 118, 121 Courtesy the artists and Lisson Gallery, London

p.103 Photograph by Stephen White. Courtesy Jay Jopling / White Cube (London)

p.119 Commissioned and produced by Artangel. Photograph by Martin Jenkinson

p.120 Photograph courtesy of greengrassi, London